The Well-Edited

Ninja CREAMI

Cookbook for Beginners

1800 Days of Irresistible Ninja CREAMI Recipes to Unleash Your Imagination and Delight Your Tastebuds with Endless Possibilities

Natasha R. Stancil

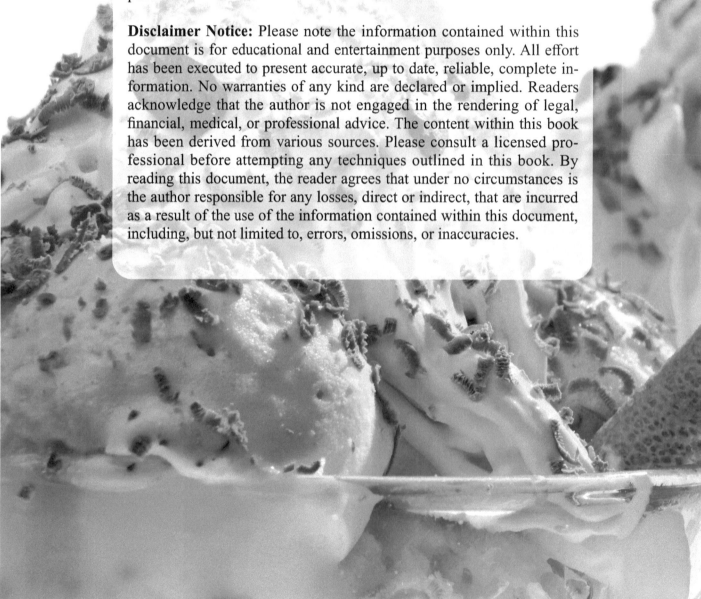

CONTENTS

Ice Cream Mix-ins Recipes 36

Smoothie Bowls Recipes 49

Sorbet Recipes 61

INTRODUCTION

Are you a foodie who loves all things creamy and frozen? Do you have a sweet tooth that just won't quit?

Look no further than the Ninja Creami Cookbook! Featuring 1800 days of mouth-watering recipes for all kinds of creamy and frozen treats, this cookbook is a must-have for anyone who loves desserts or wants to learn how to make them.

Hi, my name is Natasha R. Stancil, and I am the author of the Ninja Creami Cookbook. As a food lover and dessert enthusiast, I have always enjoyed experimenting with different flavors and textures to create delicious and unique treats. Over the years, I have collected and created countless recipes that have become family favorites. I decided to share my recipes with the world by creating this cookbook.

The Ninja Creami Cookbook is not just any ordinary dessert cookbook. It is designed specifically for the Ninja Creami, a versatile kitchen appliance that can be used to make a wide range of creamy and frozen treats, from ice cream to smoothies to milkshakes. This cookbook includes recipes for every occasion, whether you're looking for a quick and easy treat or a show-stopping dessert to impress your guests.

What sets the Ninja Creami Cookbook apart from other dessert cookbooks is the variety of recipes and the ease of use. Each recipe is written in a step-by-step format with clear instructions to guide you through the process. The recipes are also organized by category and labeled with icons to make it easy to find what you're looking for. The cookbook also includes tips and tricks for using the Ninja Creami to get the best results.

In addition to the recipes, the Ninja Creami Cookbook also includes a section on ingredient substitutions and a conversion chart for measurements. This makes it easy to adapt the recipes to suit your taste or dietary needs.

Overall, the Ninja Creami Cookbook is a must-have for anyone who loves creamy and frozen treats or wants to learn how to make them. With 1800 days of delicious recipes, clear instructions, and helpful tips, this cookbook is sure to become a staple in your kitchen. Now start creating your own creamy and frozen masterpieces!

What is the Ninja CREAMI?

The Ninja CREAMi is a kitchen appliance that allows users to make homemade ice cream, gelato, sorbet, and other frozen desserts. The machine is designed to be easy to use, and it comes with a variety of features that make it a popular choice for home cooks and dessert enthusiasts.

The Ninja CREAMi uses a special freezing bowl that is pre-frozen before use. The ingredients for the dessert are then added to the bowl, and the machine churns the mixture to create a smooth and creamy texture. The machine has a powerful motor and is designed to be able to handle hard and soft ingredients equally well.

One of the unique features of the Ninja CREAMi is its ability to make desserts quickly, with some recipes taking as little as 15 minutes. The Ice Cream Maker also has a built-in timer and automatic shut-off feature, making it easy to create perfect desserts every time.

What are the benefits of using Ninja CREAMI?

There are many benefits to using Ninja CREAMI, both in terms of its cream puffs and its ice cream maker. Here are some of the key advantages:

- High-quality ingredients

Ninja CREAMI uses only the freshest and highest-quality ingredients in its desserts. This means that you can feel good about what you're eating, knowing that you're getting a delicious treat made with real cream, eggs, and other natural ingredients.

Unique flavors

Ninja CREAMI is known for its creative and innovative flavors of cream puffs and ice cream. Whether you're in the mood for classic vanilla or something more exotic like matcha or black sesame, you're sure to find a flavor that you love.

Convenience

With Ninja CREAMI's ice cream maker, you can make homemade frozen desserts quickly and easily in the comfort of your own home. You don't need any special skills or equipment, and the machine does most of the work for you.

Customization

One of the benefits of making your own ice cream and other frozen desserts is that you can customize the flavors and ingredients to your liking. With Ninja CREAMI, you can experiment with different flavor combinations and create a dessert that is truly unique.

Healthier options

While many desserts can be high in calories and sugar, Ninja CREAMI offers some healthier options that are lower in fat and calories. For example, their sorbets are made with fruit and contain no dairy, making them a great choice for anyone who is lactose intolerant or trying to cut back on dairy.

Fun and creative

Making your own ice cream and cream puffs can be a fun and creative activity for the whole family. Whether you're experimenting with new flavors or decorating your cream puffs with colorful toppings, Ninja CREAMI offers a fun and delicious way to get creative in the kitchen.

How to clean the Ninja CREAMI?

Cleaning the Ninja CREAMI ice cream maker is quick and easy, and should be done after each use to keep the appliance in good condition. Here are the steps to follow for cleaning the ice cream maker:

1. Unplug the machine: Before cleaning the Ninja CREAMI, make sure to unplug the machine and let it cool down completely.

2. Remove the bowl: Take out the freezing bowl from the machine and rinse it under cold water to remove any remaining ice cream or other frozen dessert. Do not use hot water, as this can damage the bowl.

3. Wash the bowl: Wash the bowl in a mixture of warm water and a mild detergent, using a soft cloth or sponge to remove any remaining residue. Avoid using abrasive cleaners or scrubbers, as these can scratch the surface of the bowl.

4. Rinse the bowl: Rinse the bowl thoroughly with clean water to remove any soap or detergent. Make sure to remove all the soap residue, as this can affect the taste of the next batch of ice cream.

5. Dry the bowl: Dry the bowl with a clean, soft cloth or allow it to air dry completely before storing it back in the freezer.

6. Clean the outer surface: Use a damp cloth to wipe down the outer surface of the machine, taking care not to get any water or cleaning solution inside the machine.

7. Store the machine: Once the machine is dry, store it in a cool, dry place until the next use.

It's important to note that the paddle and lid of the machine are not dishwasher safe, so they should be washed by hand in warm, soapy water and dried thoroughly before storing. Following these simple steps will help keep your Ninja CREAMI ice cream maker clean and in good condition for years to come.

Measurement Conversions

BASIC KITCHEN CONVERSIONS & EQUIVALENTS

DRY MEASUREMENTS CONVERSION CHART

3 TEASPOONS = 1 TABLESPOON = 1/16 CUP

6 TEASPOONS = 2 TABLESPOONS = 1/8 CUP

12 TEASPOONS = 4 TABLESPOONS = 1/4 CUP

24 TEASPOONS = 8 TABLESPOONS = 1/2 CUP

36 TEASPOONS = 12 TABLESPOONS = 3/4 CUP

48 TEASPOONS = 16 TABLESPOONS = 1 CUP

METRIC TO US COOKING CONVERSIONS

OVEN TEMPERATURES

120 °C = 250 °F

160 °C = 320 °F

180° C = 350 °F

205 °C = 400 °F

220 °C = 425 °F

LIQUID MEASUREMENTS CONVERSION CHART

8 FLUID OUNCES = 1 CUP = 1/2 PINT = 1/4 QUART

16 FLUID OUNCES = 2 CUPS = 1 PINT = 1/2 QUART

32 FLUID OUNCES = 4 CUPS = 2 PINTS = 1 QUART = 1/4 GALLON

128 FLUID OUNCES = 16 CUPS = 8 PINTS = 4 QUARTS = 1 GALLON

BAKING IN GRAMS

1 CUP FLOUR = 140 GRAMS

1 CUP SUGAR = 150 GRAMS

1 CUP POWDERED SUGAR = 160 GRAMS

1 CUP HEAVY CREAM = 235 GRAMS

VOLUME

1 MILLILITER = 1/5 TEASPOON

5 ML = 1 TEASPOON

15 ML = 1 TABLESPOON

240 ML = 1 CUP OR 8 FLUID OUNCES

1 LITER = 34 FL. OUNCES

WEIGHT

1 GRAM = .035 OUNCES

100 GRAMS = 3.5 OUNCES

500 GRAMS = 1.1 POUNDS

1 KILOGRAM = 35 OUNCES

US TO METRIC COOKING CONVERSIONS

1/5 TSP = 1 ML

1 TSP = 5 ML

1 TBSP = 15 ML

1 FL OUNCE = 30 ML

1 CUP = 237 ML

1 PINT (2 CUPS) = 473 ML

1 QUART (4 CUPS) = .95 LITER

1 GALLON (16 CUPS) = 3.8 LITERS

1 OZ = 28 GRAMS

1 POUND = 454 GRAMS

BUTTER

1 CUP BUTTER = 2 STICKS = 8 OUNCES = 230 GRAMS = 8 TABLESPOONS

WHAT DOES 1 CUP EQUAL

1 CUP = 8 FLUID OUNCES

1 CUP = 16 TABLESPOONS

1 CUP = 48 TEASPOONS

1 CUP = 1/2 PINT

1 CUP = 1/4 QUART

1 CUP = 1/16 GALLON

1 CUP = 240 ML

BAKING PAN CONVERSIONS

1 CUP ALL-PURPOSE FLOUR = 4.5 OZ

1 CUP ROLLED OATS = 3 OZ 1 LARGE EGG = 1.7 OZ

1 CUP BUTTER = 8 OZ 1 CUP MILK = 8 OZ

1 CUP HEAVY CREAM = 8.4 OZ

1 CUP GRANULATED SUGAR = 7.1 OZ

1 CUP PACKED BROWN SUGAR = 7.75 OZ

1 CUP VEGETABLE OIL = 7.7 OZ

1 CUP UNSIFTED POWDERED SUGAR = 4.4 OZ

BAKING PAN CONVERSIONS

9-INCH ROUND CAKE PAN = 12 CUPS

10-INCH TUBE PAN = 16 CUPS

11-INCH BUNDT PAN = 12 CUPS

9-INCH SPRINGFORM PAN = 10 CUPS

9 X 5 INCH LOAF PAN = 8 CUPS

9-INCH SQUARE PAN = 8 CUPS

Gelato Recipes

Gelato Recipes

Peanut Butter Gelato

Servings: 4 | Cooking Time: 10 Minutes

Ingredients:
- 1½ C. unsweetened coconut milk
- 6 tbsp. sugar
- 1 tbsp. cornstarch
- 3 tbsp. peanut butter
- 3 dark chocolate peanut butter C., cut each into 8 pieces
- 2 tbsp. peanuts, chopped

Directions:
1. In a small saucepan, add the coconut milk, sugar, and cornstarch and mix well.
2. Place the saucepan over medium heat and bring to a boil, beating continuously.
3. Reduce the heat to low and simmer for about 3-4 minutes.
4. Remove from the heat and stir in the peanut butter.
5. Transfer the mixture into an empty Ninja CREAMi pint container.
6. Place the container into an ice bath to cool.
7. After cooling, cover the container with the storage lid and freeze for 24 hours.
8. After 24 hours, remove the lid from container and arrange into the outer bowl of Ninja CREAMi.
9. Install the "Creamerizer Paddle" onto the lid of outer bowl.
10. Then rotate the lid clockwise to lock.
11. Press "Power" button to turn on the unit.
12. Then press "GELATO" button.
13. When the program is completed, with a spoon, create a 1½-inch wide hole in the center that reaches the bottom of the pint container.
14. Add the peanut butter C. and peanuts into the hole and press "MIX-IN" button.
15. When the program is completed, turn the outer bowl and release it from the machine.
16. Transfer the gelato into serving bowls and serve immediately.

Nutrition Info:
- InfoCalories: 426,Carbohydrates: 34.2g,Protein: 6.8g,Fat: 29.7g,Sodium: 124m.

Orange Sherbet

Servings:4 | Cooking Time:x

Ingredients:
- 1 cup orange juice
- ¼ cup plus 1 tablespoon granulated sugar
- ¼ cup whole milk
- ½ cup heavy (whipping) cream

Directions:
1. In a large bowl, whisk together the orange juice, sugar, milk, and heavy cream until everything is well combined and the sugar is dissolved.
2. Pour the base into a clean CREAMi Pint. Place the storage lid on the container and freeze for 24 hours.
3. Remove the pint from the freezer and take off the lid. Place the pint in the outer bowl of your Ninja CREAMi, install the Creamerizer Paddle in the outer bowl lid, and lock the lid assembly onto the outer bowl. Place the bowl assembly on the motor base, and twist the handle to the right to raise the platform and lock it in place. Select the Ice Cream function.
4. Once the machine has finished processing, remove the sherbet from the pint. Serve immediately with desired toppings.

Squash Gelato

Servings: 4 | Cooking Time: 5 Minutes

Ingredients:

- 1¾ C. milk
- ½ C. cooked butternut squash
- ¼ C. granulated sugar
- ½ tsp. ground cinnamon
- ¼ tsp. ground allspice
- Pinch of salt

Directions:

1. In a small saucepan, add all ingredients and beat until well combined.
2. Place the saucepan over medium heat and cook for about 5 minutes, stirring continuously.
3. Remove from the heat and transfer the mixture into an empty Ninja CREAMi pint container.
4. Place the container into an ice bath to cool.
5. After cooling, cover the container with the storage lid and freeze for 24 hours.
6. After 24 hours, remove the lid from container and arrange into the outer bowl of Ninja CREAMi.
7. Install the "Creamerizer Paddle" onto the lid of outer bowl.
8. Then rotate the lid clockwise to lock.
9. Press "Power" button to turn on the unit.
10. Then press "GELATO" button.
11. When the program is completed, turn the outer bowl and release it from the machine.
12. Transfer the gelato into serving bowls and serve immediately.

Nutrition Info:

InfoCalories: 109,Carbohydrates: 20.1g,Protein: 3.7g,Fat: 2.2g,Sodium: 90m.

Marshmallow Cookie Gelato

Servings: 4 | Cooking Time: 6 Minutes

Ingredients:

- 1 whole vanilla bean, split in half lengthwise, scraped
- 4 egg yolks
- ¾ C. heavy cream
- 1/3 C. whole milk
- 2 tbsp. granulated sugar
- 1 tbsp. light corn syrup
- 1 tsp. vanilla extract
- 5 tbsp. marshmallow paste
- 5 peanut butter cookies, chopped

Directions:

1. In a medium saucepan, add the vanilla bean over medium-high heat, and toast for about 2-3 minutes, stirring continuously.
2. Reduce the heat to medium-low and whisk in the egg yolks, heavy cream, milk, sugar, corn syrup and vanilla extract.
3. Cook for about 2-3 minutes, stirring continuously.
4. Remove from the heat and through a fine-mesh strainer, strain the mixture into an empty Ninja CREAMi pint container.
5. Place the container into an ice bath to cool.
6. After cooling, cover the container with the storage lid and freeze for 24 hours.
7. After 24 hours, remove the lid from container and arrange into the outer bowl of Ninja CREAMi.
8. Install the "Creamerizer Paddle" onto the lid of outer bowl.
9. Then rotate the lid clockwise to lock.
10. Press "Power" button to turn on the unit.
11. Then press "GELATO" button.
12. When the program is completed, with a spoon, create a 1½-inch wide hole in the center that reaches the bottom of the pint container.
13. Add the cookies into the hole and press "MIX-IN" button.
14. When the program is completed, turn the outer bowl and release it from the machine.
15. Transfer the gelato into serving bowls and serve immediately.

Nutrition Info:

InfoCalories: 345,Carbohydrates: 31.9g,Protein: 6.3g,Fat: 21g,Sodium: 103m.

Caramel Egg Gelato

Servings: 4 | Cooking Time: 10 Minutes

Ingredients:
- ¼ C. agave nectar
- ¾ C. unsweetened soy milk
- ½ C. unsweetened creamer
- 2 eggs
- 3 tbsp. granulated sugar
- ¼ C. caramels, chopped

Directions:
1. In a medium saucepan, add agave nectar over medium-high heat and cook for about 2-3 minutes.
2. Remove the saucepan from heat and slowly whisk in the soy milk and creamer.
3. Return the pan over medium-high heat and whisk in the eggs and sugar.
4. Cook for about 4-5 minutes, stirring frequently.
5. Remove from the heat and through a fine-mesh strainer, strain the mixture into an empty Ninja CREAMi pint container.
6. Place the container into an ice bath to cool.
7. After cooling, cover the container with the storage lid and freeze for 24 hours.
8. After 24 hours, remove the lid from container and arrange into the outer bowl of Ninja CREAMi.
9. Install the "Creamerizer Paddle" onto the lid of outer bowl.
10. Then rotate the lid clockwise to lock.
11. Press "Power" button to turn on the unit.
12. Then press "GELATO" button.
13. When the program is completed, with a spoon, create a 1½-inch wide hole in the center that reaches the bottom of the pint container.
14. Add the chopped caramels into the hole and press "MIX-IN" button.
15. When the program is completed, turn the outer bowl and release it from the machine.
16. Transfer the gelato into serving bowls and serve immediately.

Nutrition Info:
- InfoCalories: 174,Carbohydrates: 29.8g,Protein: 4.6g,Fat: 4.8g,Sodium: 66m.

Tiramisu Gelato

Servings:4 | Cooking Time:x

Ingredients:
- 4 large egg yolks
- ⅓ cup granulated sugar
- 1 cup whole milk
- ⅓ cup heavy (whipping) cream
- ¼ cup cream cheese
- 1 tablespoon instant coffee
- 1 teaspoon rum extract
- ¼ cup ladyfinger pieces

Directions:
1. Fill a large bowl with ice water and set it aside.
2. In a small saucepan, whisk together the egg yolks and sugar until the mixture is fully combined and the sugar is dissolved. Do not do this over heat.
3. Whisk in the milk, heavy cream, cream cheese, instant coffee, and rum extract.
4. Place the pan over medium heat. Cook, stirring constantly with a rubber spatula, until the temperature reaches 165°F to 175°F on an instant-read thermometer.
5. Remove the pan from the heat and pour the base through a fine-mesh strainer into a clean CREAMi Pint. Carefully place the container in the prepared ice water bath, making sure the water doesn't spill into the base.
6. Once the base has cooled, place the storage lid on the pint and freeze for 24 hours.
7. Remove the pint from the freezer and take off the lid. Place the pint in the outer bowl of your Ninja CREAMi, install the Creamerizer Paddle in the outer bowl lid, and lock the lid assembly onto the outer bowl. Place the bowl assembly on the motor base, and twist the handle to the right to raise the platform and lock it in place. Select the Gelato function.
8. Once the machine has finished processing, remove the lid from the pint container. With a spoon, create a 1½-inch-wide hole that reaches the bottom of the pint. During this process, it is okay if your treat reaches above the Max Fill line. Add the ladyfinger pieces to the hole in the pint, replace the lid, and select the Mix-In function.
9. Once the machine has finished processing, remove the gelato from the pint. Serve immediately.

Servings:4 | Cooking Time:x

ngredients:
- 1 cup whole milk, divided
- 1 tablespoon, plus ¼ cup cornstarch
- ½ cup heavy (whipping) cream
- 1 teaspoon vanilla extract
- ⅓ cup, plus ¾ cup granulated sugar
- ½ cup raspberries
- 4 tablespoons water, divided
- ¼ cup white chocolate chips

Directions:
1. Fill a large bowl with ice water and set it aside.
2. In a small bowl, mix together ⅓ cup of milk and 1 tablespoon of cornstarch; set aside.
3. In a small saucepan, combine the remaining ⅔ cup of milk, the heavy cream, vanilla, and ⅓ cup of sugar. Whisk thoroughly to combine.
4. Place the pan over medium-high heat and bring the mixture to a simmer for about 4 minutes. Whisk in the cornstarch slurry and continue whisking constantly for about 1 minute.
5. Remove the pan from the heat and pour the base through a fine-mesh strainer into a clean CREAMi Pint. Carefully place the container in the prepared ice water bath, making sure the water doesn't spill into the base.
6. While the base chills, place the raspberries, remaining ¾ cup of sugar, and 2 tablespoons of water in a small saucepan. Place the pan over medium heat. Cook, stirring constantly, for about 5 minutes, until the mixture is bubbling and the raspberries have broken down.
7. In a small bowl, whisk together the remaining 2 tablespoons of water and ¼ cup of cornstarch. Pour this mixture into the raspberry liquid. Continue to cook, stirring until the mixture has thickened, about 1 minute. Pour the raspberry mixture into a clean container, then carefully place the container in the ice water bath, making sure the water doesn't spill inside the container.
8. Once the base and raspberry mixtures are cold, carefully fold the raspberry mixture into the gelato base. Pour this mixture back into the CREAMi Pint, place the storage lid on the container, and freeze for 24 hours.
9. Remove the pint from the freezer and take off the lid. Place the pint in the outer bowl of your Ninja CREAMi, install the Creamerizer Paddle in the outer bowl lid, and lock the lid assembly onto the outer bowl. Place the bowl assembly on the motor base, and twist the handle to the right to raise the platform and lock it in place. Select the Gelato function.
10. Once the machine has finished processing, remove the lid from the pint. With a spoon, create a 1½-inch-wide hole that reaches the bottom of the pint. During this process, it is okay if your treat reaches above the Max Fill line. Add the white chocolate chips to the hole in the pint, replace the lid, and select the Mix-In function.
11. Once the machine has finished processing, remove the gelato from the pint. Serve immediately with desired toppings.

Maple Gelato

Ingredients:
- 4 large egg yolks
- ½ C. plus 1 tbsp. light brown sugar
- 1 tbsp. maple syrup
- 1 tsp. maple extract
- 1 C. whole milk
- 1/3 C. heavy cream

Directions:
1. In a small saucepan, add the egg yolks, brown sugar, maple syrup and maple extract and beat until well combined.
2. Add the milk and heavy cream and beat until well combined.
3. Place the saucepan over medium heat and cook for about 2-3 minutes, stirring continuously.
4. Remove from the heat and through a fine-mesh strainer, strain the mixture into an empty Ninja CREAMi pint container.
5. Place the container into an ice bath to cool.
6. After cooling, cover the container with the storage lid and freeze for 24 hours.
7. After 24 hours, remove the lid from container and arrange into the outer bowl of Ninja CREAMi.
8. Install the "Creamerizer Paddle" onto the lid of outer bowl.
9. Then rotate the lid clockwise to lock.
10. Press "Power" button to turn on the unit.
11. Then press "GELATO" button.
12. When the program is completed, turn the outer bowl and release it from the machine.
13. Transfer the gelato into serving bowls and serve immediately.

Nutrition Info:
- InfoCalories: 218,Carbohydrates: 27g,Protein: 4.9g,Fat: 10.2g,Sodium: 43m.

Red Velvet Gelato

Servings:4 | Cooking Time:x

Ingredients:
- 4 large egg yolks
- ¼ cup granulated sugar
- 2 tablespoons unsweetened cocoa powder
- 1 cup whole milk
- ⅓ cup heavy (whipping) cream
- ¼ cup cream cheese, at room temperature
- 1 teaspoon vanilla extract
- 1 teaspoon red food coloring

Directions:
1. Fill a large bowl with ice water and set it aside.
2. In a small saucepan, whisk together the egg yolks, sugar, and cocoa powder until everything is fully combined and the sugar is dissolved. Do not do this over heat.
3. Whisk in the milk, heavy cream, cream cheese, vanilla, and food coloring.
4. Place the pan over medium heat. Cook, stirring constantly with a rubber spatula, until the temperature reaches 165°F to 175°F on an instant-read thermometer.
5. Remove the pan from the heat and pour the base through a fine-mesh strainer into a clean CREAMi Pint. Carefully place the container in the prepared ice water bath, making sure the water doesn't spill into the base.
6. Once the base has cooled, place the storage lid on the pint and freeze for 24 hours.
7. Remove the pint from the freezer and take off the lid. Place the pint in the outer bowl of your Ninja CREAMi, install the Creamerizer Paddle in the outer bowl lid, and lock the lid assembly onto the outer bowl. Place the bowl assembly on the motor base, and twist the handle to the right to raise the platform and lock it in place. Select the Gelato function.
8. Once the machine has finished processing, remove the gelato from the pint. Serve immediately.

Chocolate Cauliflower Gelato

Servings: 4 | Cooking Time: 3 Minutes

Ingredients:

1 C. whole milk
½ C. heavy cream
1/3 C. sugar
2 tbsp. cocoa powder

- ½ C. frozen cauliflower rice
- ¼ tsp. almond extract
- Pinch of salt
- ½ C. dark chocolate, chopped

Directions:

1. In a small saucepan, add all ingredients except for chopped chocolate and beat until well combined.
2. Place the saucepan over medium heat and cook for about 2-3 minutes, stirring continuously.
3. Remove from the heat and transfer the mixture into an empty Ninja CREAMi pint container.
4. Place the container into an ice bath to cool.
5. After cooling, cover the container with the storage lid and freeze for 24 hours.
6. After 24 hours, remove the lid from container and arrange into the outer bowl of Ninja CREAMi.
7. Install the "Creamerizer Paddle" onto the lid of outer bowl.
8. Then rotate the lid clockwise to lock.
9. Press "Power" button to turn on the unit.
10. Then press "GELATO" button.
11. When the program is completed, with a spoon, create a 1½-inch wide hole in the center that reaches the bottom of the pint container.
12. Add the chopped chocolate into the hole and press "MIX-IN" button.
13. When the program is completed, turn the outer bowl and release it from the machine.
14. Transfer the gelato into serving bowls and serve immediately.

Nutrition Info:

- InfoCalories: 273,Carbohydrates: 34.5g,Protein: 4.6g,Fat: 14.1g,Sodium: 90m.

Vanilla Bean Gelato

Servings:4 | Cooking Time:x

Ingredients:

- 4 large egg yolks
- 1 tablespoon light corn syrup
- ¼ cup plus 1 tablespoon granulated sugar
- ⅓ cup whole milk
- 1 cup heavy (whipping) cream
- 1 whole vanilla bean, split in half lengthwise and scraped

Directions:

1. Fill a large bowl with ice water and set it aside.
2. In a small saucepan, whisk together the egg yolks, corn syrup, and sugar until everything is fully combined and the sugar is dissolved. Do not do this over heat.
3. Whisk in the milk, heavy cream, and vanilla bean scrapings (discard the pod).
4. Place the pan over medium heat. Cook, stirring constantly with a rubber spatula, until the temperature reaches 165°F to 175°F on an instant-read thermometer.
5. Remove the pan from the heat and pour the base through a fine-mesh strainer into a clean CREAMi Pint. Carefully place the container in the prepared ice water bath, making sure the water doesn't spill into the base.
6. Once the base has cooled, place the storage lid on the pint and freeze for 24 hours.
7. Remove the pint from the freezer and take off the lid. Place the pint in the outer bowl of your Ninja CREAMi, install the Creamerizer Paddle in the outer bowl lid, and lock the lid assembly onto the outer bowl. Place the bowl assembly on the motor base, and twist the handle to the right to raise the platform and lock it in place. Select the Gelato function.
8. Once the machine has finished processing, remove the gelato from the pint. Serve immediately with desired toppings.

Chocolate Hazelnut Gelato

Servings: 4 | Cooking Time: 3 Minutes

Ingredients:
- 3 large egg yolks
- 1/3 C. hazelnut spread
- ¼ C. granulated sugar
- 2 tsp. cocoa powder
- 1 tbsp. light corn syrup
- 1 C. whole milk
- ½ C. heavy cream
- 1 tsp. vanilla extract

Directions:
1. In a small saucepan, add the egg yolks, hazelnut spread, sugar, cocoa powder and corn syrup and beat until well combined.
2. Add the milk, heavy cream and vanilla extract and beat until well combined.
3. Place the saucepan over medium heat and cook for about 2-3 minutes, stirring continuously.
4. Remove from the heat and through a fine-mesh strainer, strain the mixture into an empty Ninja CREAMi pint container.
5. Place the container into an ice bath to cool.
6. After cooling, cover the container with the storage lid and freeze for 24 hours.
7. After 24 hours, remove the lid from container and arrange into the outer bowl of Ninja CREAMi.
8. Install the "Creamerizer Paddle" onto the lid of outer bowl.
9. Then rotate the lid clockwise to lock.
10. Press "Power" button to turn on the unit.
11. Then press "GELATO" button.
12. When the program is completed, turn the outer bowl and release it from the machine.
13. Transfer the gelato into serving bowls and serve immediately.

Nutrition Info:
- InfoCalories: 321,Carbohydrates: 33.7g,Protein: 5.9g,Fat: 19g,Sodium: 50m.

Apple Cider Sorbet

Servings:4 | Cooking Time:x

Ingredients:
- 1 cup apple cider
- 1 cup applesauce
- 2 tablespoons organic sugar

Directions:
1. In a large bowl, whisk together the apple cider, applesauce, and sugar until the sugar is dissolved.
2. Pour the base into a clean CREAMi Pint. Place the storage lid on the container and freeze for 24 hours.
3. Remove the pint from the freezer and take off the lid. Place the pint in the outer bowl of your Ninja CREAMi, install the Creamerizer Paddle in the outer bowl lid, and lock the lid assembly onto the outer bowl. Place the bowl assembly on the motor base, and twist the handle to the right to raise the platform and lock it in place. Select the Sorbet function.
4. Once the machine has finished processing, remove the sorbet from the pint. Serve immediately.

Servings:4 | Cooking Time:x

Ingredients:
- NUT-FREE, FAMILY FAVORITE
- PREP TIME: 5 minutes / Cook time: 7 to 10 minutes / Freeze time: 24 hours
- FUNCTIONS: Gelato and Mix-In
- TOOLS NEEDED: Large bowl, small saucepan, whisk, rubber spatula, instant-read thermometer, fine-mesh strainer, spoon
- 4 large egg yolks
- 3 tablespoons granulated sugar
- 1 cup whole milk
- ⅓ cup heavy (whipping) cream
- ¼ cup cream cheese, at room temperature
- 1 teaspoon vanilla extract
- 3 tablespoons strawberry jam
- ¼ cup graham cracker pieces

Directions:
1. Fill a large bowl with ice water and set it aside.
2. In a small saucepan, whisk together the egg yolks and sugar until the mixture is smooth and the sugar is dissolved. Do not do this over heat.
3. Whisk in the milk, heavy cream, cream cheese, vanilla, and strawberry jam.
4. Place the pan over medium heat. Cook, stirring constantly with a rubber spatula, until the temperature reaches 165°F to 175°F on an instant-read thermometer.
5. Remove the pan from the heat and pour the base through a fine-mesh strainer into a clean CREAMi Pint. Carefully place the container in the prepared ice water bath, making sure the water doesn't spill into the base.
6. Once the base has cooled, place the storage lid on the pint and freeze for 24 hours.
7. Remove the pint from the freezer and take off the lid. Place the pint in the outer bowl of your Ninja CREAMi, install the Creamerizer Paddle in the outer bowl lid, and lock the lid assembly onto the outer bowl. Place the bowl assembly on the motor base, and twist the handle to the right to raise the platform and lock it in place. Select the Gelato function.
8. Once the machine has finished processing, remove the lid from the pint container. With a spoon, create a 1½-inch-wide hole that reaches the bottom of the pint. During this process, it is okay if your treat reaches above the Max Fill line. Add the graham cracker pieces to the hole in the pint, replace the lid, and select the Mix-In function.
9. Once the machine has finished processing, remove the gelato from the pint. Serve immediately.

Servings: 4 | Cooking Time: 5 Minutes

Ingredients:
- 1 C. whole milk
- ½ C. heavy cream
- ¼ C. sugar
- 3 egg yolk
- Pinch of sea salt
- ¼ C. mini marshmallows

Directions:
1. Preheat the oven to broiler. Lightly grease a baking sheet.
2. Arrange the marshmallows onto the prepared baking sheet in a single layer.
3. Broil for about 5 minutes, flipping once halfway through.
4. Meanwhile, in a small saucepan, add the milk, heavy cream, sugar, egg yolks and a pinch of salt and beat until well combined.
5. Place the saucepan over medium heat and cook for about 1 minute, stirring continuously.
6. Remove from the heat and stir in half of the marshmallows.
7. Transfer the mixture into an empty Ninja CREAMi pint container.
8. Place the container into an ice bath to cool.
9. After cooling, cover the container with the storage lid and freeze for 24 hours.
10. Reserve the remaining marshmallows into the freezer.
11. After 24 hours, remove the lid from container and arrange into the outer bowl of Ninja CREAMi.
12. Install the "Creamerizer Paddle" onto the lid of outer bowl.
13. Then rotate the lid clockwise to lock.
14. Press "Power" button to turn on the unit.
15. Then press "GELATO" button.
16. When the program is completed, with a spoon, create a 1½-inch wide hole in the center that reaches the bottom of the pint container.
17. Add the reserved frozen marshmallows into the hole and press "MIX-IN" button.
18. When the program is completed, turn the outer bowl and release it from the machine.
19. Transfer the gelato into serving bowls and serve immediately.

Nutrition Info:
- InfoCalories: 186,Carbohydrates: 18.7g,Protein: 4.4g,Fat: 10.9g,Sodium: 77m.

Blueberry & Crackers Gelato

Servings: 4 | Cooking Time: 3 Minutes

ngredients:

- 4 large egg yolks
- 3 tbsp. granulated sugar
- 3 tbsp. wild blueberry preserves
- 1 tsp. vanilla extract
- 1 C. whole milk

- 1/3 C. heavy cream
- ¼ C. cream cheese, softened
- 3-6 drops purple food coloring
- 2 large graham crackers, broken in 1-inch pieces

Directions:

1. In a small saucepan, add the egg yolks, sugar, blueberry preserves and vanilla extract and beat until well combined.
2. Add the milk, heavy cream, cream cheese and food coloring and beat until well combined.
3. Place the saucepan over medium heat and cook for about 2-3 minutes, stirring continuously.
4. Remove from the heat and through a fine-mesh strainer, strain the mixture into an empty Ninja CREAMi pint container.
5. Place the container into an ice bath to cool.
6. After cooling, cover the container with the storage lid and freeze for 24 hours.
7. After 24 hours, remove the lid from container and arrange into the outer bowl of Ninja CREAMi.
8. Install the "Creamerizer Paddle" onto the lid of outer bowl.
9. Then rotate the lid clockwise to lock.
10. Press "Power" button to turn on the unit.
11. Then press "GELATO" button.
12. When the program is completed, with a spoon, create a 1½-inch wide hole in the center that reaches the bottom of the pint container.
13. Add the graham crackers into the hole and press "MIX-IN" button.
14. When the program is completed, turn the outer bowl and release it from the machine.
15. Transfer the gelato into serving bowls and serve immediately.

Nutrition Info:

- InfoCalories: 279,Carbohydrates: 28.3g,Protein: 6.4g,Fat: 16g,Sodium: 122m.

Chocolate-hazelnut Gelato

Servings:4 | Cooking Time:x

Ingredients:

- 3 large egg yolks
- ⅓ cup chocolate-hazelnut spread
- 2 teaspoons unsweetened cocoa powder
- 1 tablespoon corn syrup

- ¼ cup granulated sugar
- 1 cup whole milk
- ½ cup heavy (whipping) cream
- 1 teaspoon vanilla extract

Directions:

1. Fill a large bowl with ice water and set it aside.
2. In a small saucepan, whisk together the egg yolks, chocolate-hazelnut spread, cocoa powder, corn syrup, and sugar until the mixture is fully combined and the sugar is dissolved. Do not do this over heat.
3. Whisk in the milk, heavy cream, and vanilla.
4. Place the pan over medium heat. Cook, stirring constantly with a rubber spatula, until the temperature reaches 165°F to 175°F on an instant-read thermometer.
5. Remove the pan from the heat and pour the base through a fine-mesh strainer into a clean CREAMi Pint. Carefully place the container in the prepared ice water bath, making sure the water doesn't spill into the base.
6. Once the base has cooled, place the storage lid on the pint and freeze for 24 hours.
7. Remove the pint from the freezer and take off the lid. Place the pint in the outer bowl of your Ninja CREAMi, install the Creamerizer Paddle in the outer bowl lid, and lock the lid assembly onto the outer bowl. Place the bowl assembly on the motor base, and twist the handle to the right to raise the platform and lock it in place. Select the Gelato function.
8. Once the machine has finished processing, remove the gelato from the pint. Serve immediately with desired toppings.

Spirulina Cookie Gelato

Servings: 4 | Cooking Time: 3 Minutes

Ingredients:
- 4 large egg yolks
- 1/3 C. granulated sugar
- 1 C. oat milk
- 1 tsp. vanilla extract
- 1 tsp. blue spirulina powder
- 4 small crunchy chocolate chip cookies, crumbled

Directions:
1. In a small saucepan, add the egg yolks and sugar and beat until well combined.
2. Add oat milk and vanilla extract and stir to combine.
3. Place the saucepan over medium heat and cook for about 2-3 minutes, stirring continuously.
4. Remove from the heat and through a fine-mesh strainer, strain the mixture into an empty Ninja CREAMi pint container.
5. Place the container into an ice bath to cool.
6. After cooling, cover the container with the storage lid and freeze for 24 hours.
7. After 24 hours, remove the lid from container and arrange into the outer bowl of Ninja CREAMi.
8. Install the "Creamerizer Paddle" onto the lid of outer bowl.
9. Then rotate the lid clockwise to lock.
10. Press "Power" button to turn on the unit.
11. Then press "GELATO" button.
12. When the program is completed, with a spoon, create a 1½-inch wide hole in the center that reaches the bottom of the pint container.
13. Add the chocolate chip cookies into the hole and press "MIX-IN" button.
14. When the program is completed, turn the outer bowl and release it from the machine.
15. Transfer the gelato into serving bowls and serve immediately.

Nutrition Info:
- InfoCalories: 235,Carbohydrates: 35.4g,Protein: 4.5g,Fat: 8.9g,Sodium: 104m.

Banana & Squash Cookie Gelato

Servings: 4 | Cooking Time: 3 Minutes

Ingredients:
- 4 large egg yolks
- 1 C. heavy cream
- 1/3 C. granulated sugar
- ½ of banana, peeled and sliced
- ½ C. frozen butternut squash, chopped
- 1 box instant vanilla pudding mix
- 6 vanilla wafer cookies, crumbled

Directions:
1. In a small saucepan, add the egg yolks, heavy cream and sugar and beat until well combined.
2. Place the saucepan over medium heat and cook for about 2-3 minutes, stirring continuously.
3. Remove from the heat and through a fine-mesh strainer, strain the mixture into an empty Ninja CREAMi pint container.
4. Place the container into an ice bath to cool.
5. After cooling, add in the banana, squash and pudding until well combined.
6. Cover the container with the storage lid and freeze for 24 hours.
7. After 24 hours, remove the lid from container and arrange into the outer bowl of Ninja CREAMi.
8. Install the "Creamerizer Paddle" onto the lid of outer bowl.
9. Then rotate the lid clockwise to lock.
10. Press "Power" button to turn on the unit.
11. Then press "GELATO" button.
12. When the program is completed, with a spoon, create a 1½-inch wide hole in the center that reaches the bottom of the pint container.
13. Add the wafer cookies into the hole and press "MIX-IN" button.
14. When the program is completed, turn the outer bowl and release it from the machine.
15. Transfer the gelato into serving bowls and serve immediately.

Nutrition Info:
- InfoCalories: 489,Carbohydrates: 61.6g,Protein: 5.7g,Fat: 24.7g,Sodium: 194m.

Vanilla Gelato

Servings: 4 | Cooking Time: 3 Minutes

Ingredients:
- 4 large egg yolks
- 1 tbsp. light corn syrup
- ¼ C. plus 1 tbsp. granulated sugar
- 1 C. heavy cream
- 1/3 C. whole milk
- 1 whole vanilla bean, split in half lengthwise and scraped

Directions:
1. In a small saucepan, add the egg yolks, corn syrup and sugar and beat until well combined.
2. Add the heavy cream, milk and vanilla bean and beat until well combined.
3. Place the saucepan over medium heat and cook for about 2-3 minutes, stirring continuously.
4. Remove from the heat and through a fine-mesh strainer, strain the mixture into an empty Ninja CREAMi pint container.
5. Place the container into an ice bath to cool.
6. After cooling, cover the container with the storage lid and freeze for 24 hours.
7. After 24 hours, remove the lid from container and arrange into the outer bowl of Ninja CREAMi.
8. Install the "Creamerizer Paddle" onto the lid of outer bowl.
9. Then rotate the lid clockwise to lock.
10. Press "Power" button to turn on the unit.
11. Then press "GELATO" button.
12. When the program is completed, turn the outer bowl and release it from the machine.
13. Transfer the gelato into serving bowls and serve immediately.

Nutrition Info:
- InfoCalories: 239,Carbohydrates: 21g,Protein: 4g,Fat: 16.3g,Sodium: 28m.

Carrot Gelato

Servings: 4 | Cooking Time: 3 Minutes

Ingredients:
- 3 large egg yolks
- 1/3 C. coconut sugar
- 1 tbsp. brown rice syrup
- ½ C. heavy cream
- 1 C. unsweetened almond milk
- ½ C. carrot puree
- ½ tsp. ground cinnamon
- ¼ tsp. ground nutmeg
- ¼ tsp. ground ginger
- ¼ tsp. ground cloves
- ¾ tsp. vanilla extract

Directions:
1. In a small saucepan, add the egg yolks, coconut sugar and brown rice syrup and beat until well combined.
2. Add the heavy cream, almond milk, carrot puree and spices and beat until well combined.
3. Place the saucepan over medium heat and cook for about 2-3 minutes, stirring continuously.
4. Remove from the heat and stir in the vanilla extract.
5. Through a fine-mesh strainer, strain the mixture into an empty Ninja CREAMi pint container.
6. Place the container into an ice bath to cool.
7. After cooling, cover the container with the storage lid and freeze for 24 hours.
8. After 24 hours, remove the lid from container and arrange into the outer bowl of Ninja CREAMi.
9. Install the "Creamerizer Paddle" onto the lid of outer bowl.
10. Then rotate the lid clockwise to lock.
11. Press "Power" button to turn on the unit.
12. Then press "GELATO" button.
13. When the program is completed, turn the outer bowl and release it from the machine.
14. Transfer the gelato into serving bowls and serve immediately.

Nutrition Info:
- InfoCalories: 146,Carbohydrates: 22.7g,Protein: 0.8g,Fat: 6.5g,Sodium: 64m.

Pumpkin Gelato

Servings: 4 | Cooking Time: 3 Minutes

Ingredients:
- 3 large egg yolks
- 1/3 C. granulated sugar
- 1 tbsp. light corn syrup
- 1 C. whole milk
- ½ C. heavy cream
- ½ C. canned pumpkin puree
- 1½ tsp. pumpkin pie spice
- 1 tsp. vanilla extract

Directions:
1. In a small saucepan, add the egg yolks, sugar and corn syrup and beat until well combined.
2. Add the milk, heavy cream, pumpkin puree and pumpkin pie spice and beat until well combined.
3. Place the saucepan over medium heat and cook for about 2-3 minutes, stirring continuously.
4. Remove from the heat and stir in the vanilla extract.
5. Through a fine-mesh strainer, strain the mixture into an empty Ninja CREAMi pint container.
6. Place the container into an ice bath to cool.
7. After cooling, cover the container with the storage lid and freeze for 24 hours.
8. After 24 hours, remove the lid from container and arrange into the outer bowl of Ninja CREAMi.
9. Install the "Creamerizer Paddle" onto the lid of outer bowl.
10. Then rotate the lid clockwise to lock.
11. Press "Power" button to turn on the unit.
12. Then press "GELATO" button.
13. When the program is completed, turn the outer bowl and release it from the machine.
14. Transfer the gelato into serving bowls and serve immediately.

Nutrition Info:
- InfoCalories: 220,Carbohydrates: 27g,Protein: 4.7g,Fat: 11.1g,Sodium: 39m.

Pecan Gelato

Servings: 4 | Cooking Time: 3 Minutes

Ingredients:
- 4 large egg yolks
- 5 tbsp. granulated sugar
- 1 tbsp. light corn syrup
- 1 C. heavy cream
- 1/3 C. whole milk
- 1 tsp. butter flavor extract
- 1/3 C. pecans, chopped

Directions:
1. In a small saucepan, add the egg yolks, sugar and corn syrup and beat until well combined.
2. Add the heavy cream, milk and butter flavor extract and beat until well combined.
3. Place the saucepan over medium heat and cook for about 2-3 minutes, stirring continuously.
4. Remove from the heat and through a fine-mesh strainer, strain the mixture into an empty Ninja CREAMi pint container.
5. Place the container into an ice bath to cool.
6. After cooling, cover the container with the storage lid and freeze for 24 hours.
7. After 24 hours, remove the lid from container and arrange into the outer bowl of Ninja CREAMi.
8. Install the "Creamerizer Paddle" onto the lid of outer bowl.
9. Then rotate the lid clockwise to lock.
10. Press "Power" button to turn on the unit.
11. Then press "GELATO" button.
12. When the program is completed, with a spoon, create a 1½-inch wide hole in the center that reaches the bottom of the pint container.
13. Add the pecans into the hole and press "MIX-IN" button.
14. When the program is completed, turn the outer bowl and release it from the machine.
15. Transfer the gelato into serving bowls and serve immediately.

Nutrition Info:
- InfoCalories: 319,Carbohydrates: 22.6g,Protein: 5.2g,Fat: 24.5g,Sodium: 29m.

Milkshake Recipes

Milkshake Recipes

Lime Sherbet Milkshake

Servings: 1 | Cooking Time:x

Ingredients:
- 1½ C. rainbow sherbet
- ½ C. lime seltzer

Directions:
1. In an empty Ninja CREAMi pint container, place sherbet and top with lime seltzer.
2. Arrange the container into the outer bowl of Ninja CREAMi.
3. Install the "Creamerizer Paddle" onto the lid of outer bowl.
4. Then rotate the lid clockwise to lock.
5. Press "Power" button to turn on the unit.
6. Then press "MILKSHAKE" button.
7. When the program is completed, turn the outer bowl and release it from the machine.
8. Transfer the shake into a serving glass and serve immediately.

Nutrition Info:
- InfoCalories: 195,Carbohydrates: 40.5g,Protein: 1.5g,Fat: 2.3g,Sodium: 94m.

Dairy-free Strawberry Milkshake

Servings:2 | Cooking Time:x

Ingredients:
- 1½ cups Coconut-Vanilla Ice Cream
- ½ cup oat milk
- 3 fresh strawberries

Directions:
1. Combine the ice cream, oat milk, and strawberries in a clean CREAMi Pint.
2. Place the pint in the outer bowl of your Ninja CREAMi, install the Creamerizer Paddle in the outer bowl lid, and lock the lid assembly onto the outer bowl. Place the bowl assembly on the motor base, and twist the handle to the right to raise the platform and lock it in place. Select the Milkshake function.
3. Once the machine has finished processing, remove the milkshake from the pint. Serve immediately.

Chocolate Milkshake

Servings: 1 | Cooking Time:x

Ingredients:
- 1½ C. chocolate ice cream
- ½ C. whole milk

Directions:
1. In an empty Ninja CREAMi pint container, place ice cream, followed by milk.
2. Arrange the container into the outer bowl of Ninja CREAMi.
3. Install the "Creamerizer Paddle" onto the lid of outer bowl.
4. Then rotate the lid clockwise to lock.
5. Press "Power" button to turn on the unit.
6. Then press "MILKSHAKE" button.
7. When the program is completed, turn the outer bowl and release it from the machine.
8. Transfer the shake into a serving glass and serve immediately.

Nutrition Info:
- InfoCalories: 279,Carbohydrates: 29.5g,Protein: 7.4g,Fat: 14.5g,Sodium: 84m.

Vanilla Milkshake

Servings: 2 | Cooking Time:x

Ingredients:
- 2 cups French vanilla coffee creamer
- 1 tablespoon agave nectar
- 2 ounces vodka
- 1 tablespoon rainbow sprinkles

Directions:
1. In an empty Ninja CREAMi pint container, place all ingredients and mix well.
2. Cover the container with storage lid and freeze for 24 hours.
3. After 24 hours, remove the lid from container and arrange into the Outer Bowl of Ninja CREAMi.
4. Install the Creamerizer Paddle onto the lid of Outer Bowl.
5. Then rotate the lid clockwise to lock.
6. Press Power button to turn on the unit.
7. Then press Milkshake button.
8. When the program is completed, turn the Outer Bowl and release it from the machine.
9. Transfer the shake into serving glasses and serve immediately.

Nutrition Info:
- InfoCalories: 563,Fat: 46.3g,Carbohydrates: 16.8g,Protein: 6.5.

Healthy Strawberry Shake

Servings: 1 | Cooking Time: 10 Minutes

Ingredients:
- 1 cup milk
- 1 tablespoon honey
- ½ teaspoon vanilla extract
- ½ cup frozen strawberries

Directions:
1. Add the milk, honey, vanilla extract, and strawberries into an empty CREAMi Pint.
2. Place Pint in outer bowl, install Creamerizer Paddle onto outer bowl lid and lock the lid assembly on the outer bowl. Place the bowl assembly on the motor base and crank the lever to elevate and secure the platform in place.
3. Select MILKSHAKE.
4. Remove the milkshake from the Pint after the processing is finished.

Nutrition Info:
- InfoCalories 186,Protein 8.4g,Carbohydrate 27g,Fat 5g,Sodium 102mg.

Lemon Meringue Pie Milkshake

Servings: 1 | Cooking Time: 5 Minutes

Ingredients:
- 1 cup vanilla ice cream
- 4 tablespoons store-bought lemon curd, divided
- 4 tablespoons marshmallow topping, divided
- ½ cup Graham Crackers, broken, divided

Directions:
1. Place the ice cream in an empty CREAMi Pint.
2. Use a spoon to create a 1½-inch wide hole that reaches the bottom of the Pint. Add the remaining ingredients to the hole.
3. Place Pint in outer bowl, install Creamerizer Paddle onto outer bowl lid and lock the lid assembly on the outer bowl. Place the bowl assembly on the motor base and crank the lever to elevate and secure the platform in place.
4. Select the MILKSHAKE option.
5. Remove the milkshake from the Pint after the processing is finished.

Nutrition Info:
- InfoCalories 106,Protein 4g,Carbohydrate 14g,Fat 5g,Sodium 56mg.

Boozy Amaretto Cookie Milkshake

Servings:4 | Cooking Time:x

Ingredients:
- 1 cup whole milk
- ½ cup amaretto-flavored coffee creamer
- ¼ cup amaretto liqueur
- 1 tablespoon agave nectar
- ¼ cup chopped chocolate chip cookies

Directions:
1. In a clean CREAMi Pint, combine the milk, coffee creamer, amaretto liqueur, and agave. Stir well. Place the storage lid on the container and freeze for 24 hours.
2. Remove the pint from the freezer and take off the lid. Add the chocolate chip cookies to the top of the pint. Place the pint in the outer bowl of your Ninja CREAMi, install the Creamerizer Paddle in the outer bowl lid, and lock the lid assembly onto the outer bowl. Place the bowl assembly on the motor base, and twist the handle to the right to raise the platform and lock it in place. Select the Milkshake function.
3. Once the machine has finished processing, remove the lid. With a spoon, create a 1½-inch-wide hole that reaches the bottom of the pint. During this process, it is okay if your treat reaches above the Max Fill line. Add the chopped cookies to the hole in the pint, replace the lid, and select Milkshake. Serve immediately.

Chocolate Ice Cream Milkshake

Servings: 1 | Cooking Time:x

Ingredients:
- 1½ cups chocolate ice cream
- ½ cup whole milk

Directions:
1. In an empty Ninja CREAMi pint container, place ice cream, followed by milk.
2. Arrange the container into the Outer Bowl of Ninja CREAMi.
3. Install the Creamerizer Paddle onto the lid of Outer Bowl.
4. Then rotate the lid clockwise to lock.
5. Press Power button to turn on the unit.
6. Then press Milkshake button.
7. When the program is completed, turn the Outer Bowl and release it from the machine.
8. Transfer the shake into a serving glass and serve immediately.

Nutrition Info:
- InfoCalories: 279,Fat: 14.5g,Carbohydrates: 29.5g,Protein: 7.4.

Lemon Cookie Milkshake

Servings: 2 | Cooking Time:x

Ingredients:
- 1½ cups vanilla ice cream
- 3 lemon cream sandwich cookies
- ¼ cup milk

Directions:
1. In an empty Ninja CREAMi pint container, place ice cream followed by cookies and milk.
2. Arrange the container into the Outer Bowl of Ninja CREAMi.
3. Install the Creamerizer Paddle onto the lid of Outer Bowl.
4. Then rotate the lid clockwise to lock.
5. Press Power button to turn on the unit.
6. Then press Milkshake button.
7. When the program is completed, turn the Outer Bowl and release it from the machine.
8. Transfer the shake into serving glasses and serve immediately.

Nutrition Info:
- InfoCalories: 222,Fat: 10g,Carbohydrates: 29.1g,Protein: 3.8.

Frozen Mudslide

Servings:2 | Cooking Time:x

Ingredients:
- 2 cups ice cubes
- ½ cup store-bought vanilla ice cream
- 6 tablespoons espresso vodka
- 6 tablespoons coffee-flavored liqueur
- 6 tablespoons Irish cream–flavored liqueur

Directions:
1. Combine the ice, ice cream, vodka, and liqueurs in a blender. Blend on high until smooth.
2. Pour the base into a clean CREAMi Pint. Place the storage lid on the container and freeze for 24 hours.
3. Remove the pint from the freezer and take off the lid. Place the pint in the outer bowl of your Ninja CREAMi, install the Creamerizer Paddle in the outer bowl lid, and lock the lid assembly onto the outer bowl. Place the bowl assembly on the motor base, and twist the handle to the right to raise the platform and lock it in place. Select the Milkshake function.
4. Once the machine has finished processing, remove the milkshake from the pint. Serve immediately.

Lite Peanut Butter Ice Cream

Servings:4 | Cooking Time:x

Ingredients:
- 1¾ cups fat-free (skim) milk
- ¼ cup stevia–cane sugar blend
- 1 teaspoon vanilla extract
- 3 tablespoons smooth peanut butter

Directions:
1. In a medium bowl, whisk together the milk, stevia blend, vanilla extract, and peanut butter until the mixture is smooth and the stevia is fully dissolved. Let the mixture sit for about 5 minutes, until any foam subsides. If the stevia is still not dissolved, whisk again.
2. Pour the base into a clean CREAMi Pint. Place the storage lid on the container and freeze for 24 hours.
3. Remove the pint from the freezer and take off the lid. Place the pint in the outer bowl of your Ninja CREAMi, install the Creamerizer Paddle in the outer bowl lid, and lock the lid assembly onto the outer bowl. Place the bowl assembly on the motor base, and twist the handle to the right to raise the platform and lock it in place. Select the Lite Ice Cream function.
4. Once the machine has finished processing, remove the ice cream from the pint. Serve immediately.

Chocolate Protein Milkshake

Servings: 2 | Cooking Time:x

Ingredients:
- 1 C. frozen chocolate yogurt
- 1 scoop chocolate whey protein powder
- 1 C. whole milk

Directions:
1. In an empty Ninja CREAMi pint container, place yogurt, followed by protein powder and milk.
2. Arrange the container into the outer bowl of Ninja CREAMi.
3. Install the "Creamerizer Paddle" onto the lid of outer bowl.
4. Then rotate the lid clockwise to lock.
5. Press "Power" button to turn on the unit.
6. Then press "MILKSHAKE" button.
7. When the program is completed, turn the outer bowl and release it from the machine.
8. Transfer the shake into serving glasses and serve immediately.

Nutrition Info:
- InfoCalories: 242,Carbohydrates: 30.7g,Protein: 18.6g,Fat: 4.8g,Sodium: 104m.

Orange Milkshake

Servings: 1 | Cooking Time: 5 Minutes

Ingredients:
- 1 cup orange juice
- 2 scoops vanilla ice cream
- ½ cup milk
- 2 teaspoons white sugar

Directions:
1. Place orange juice, ice cream, milk, and sugar in an empty CREAMi Pint.
2. Place Pint in outer bowl, install Creamerizer Paddle onto outer bowl lid and lock the lid assembly on the outer bowl. Place the bowl assembly on the motor base and crank the lever to elevate and secure the platform in place.
3. Select MILKSHAKE.
4. Remove the milkshake from the Pint after the processing is finished.

Nutrition Info:
- InfoCalories 346,Protein 8g,Carbohydrate 62g,Fat 7.8g,Sodium 87.3mg.

Peanut Butter Brownie Milkshake

Servings: 2 | Cooking Time: 5 Minutes

Ingredients:
- ½ cup chocolate ice cream
- ½ cup whole milk
- 2 tablespoons peanut butter, for mix-in
- 1¼ cups brownies, chopped into bite-sized pieces, for mix-in

Directions:
1. Place the ice cream in an empty CREAMi Pint.
2. Use a spoon to create a 1½-inch wide hole that reaches the bottom of the Pint. Add the remaining ingredients to the hole.
3. Place Pint in outer bowl, install Creamerizer Paddle onto outer bowl lid and lock the lid assembly on the outer bowl. Place the bowl assembly on the motor base and crank the lever to elevate and secure the platform in place.
4. Select MILKSHAKE.
5. Remove the milkshake from the Pint after the processing is finished.

Nutrition Info:
- InfoCalories 596,Protein 5g,Carbohydrate 38g,Fat 1g,Sodium 106mg.

Servings: 2 | Cooking Time: 10 Minutes

Ingredients:
- 1 cup chocolate ice cream
- ½ cup whole milk
- ¼ cup hazelnut spread

Directions:
1. Place the ice cream in an empty CREAMi Pint.
2. Create a 1½-inch-wide hole in the bottom of the Pint using a spoon. Fill the hole with the remaining ingredients.
3. Place Pint in outer bowl, install Creamerizer Paddle onto outer bowl lid and lock the lid assembly on the outer bowl. Place bowl assembly on motor base and twist the handle right to raise the platform and lock in place.
4. Select MILKSHAKE.
5. When the milkshake has finished processing, take it from the Pint and serve right away.

Nutrition Info:
- InfoCalories 516,Protein 10g,Carbohydrate 70g,Fat 22g,Sodium 200mg.

Cacao Matcha Milkshake

Servings: 2 | Cooking Time:x

Ingredients:
- 1½ C. vanilla ice cream
- ½ C. canned full-fat coconut milk
- 1 tsp. matcha powder
- ¼ C. cacao nibs
- ¾ tsp. peppermint extract
- ¼ tsp. vanilla extract

Directions:
1. In an empty Ninja CREAMi pint container, place ice cream, followed by coconut milk, matcha powder, cacao nibs and peppermint extract.
2. Arrange the container into the outer bowl of Ninja CREAMi.
3. Install the "Creamerizer Paddle" onto the lid of outer bowl.
4. Then rotate the lid clockwise to lock.
5. Press "Power" button to turn on the unit.
6. Then press "MILKSHAKE" button.
7. When the program is completed, turn the outer bowl and release it from the machine.
8. Transfer the shake into serving glasses and serve immediately.

Nutrition Info:
- InfoCalories: 363,Carbohydrates: 26.8g,Protein: 5.4g,Fat: 21.6g,Sodium: 120m.

Banana Milkshake

Servings: 2 | Cooking Time:x

Ingredients:
- 1 scoop vanilla ice cream
- 2 small bananas, peeled and halved
- 7 fluid ounces semi-skimmed milk

Directions:
1. In an empty Ninja CREAMi pint container, place ice cream followed by bananas and milk.
2. Arrange the container into the Outer Bowl of Ninja CREAMi.
3. Install the Creamerizer Paddle onto the lid of Outer Bowl.
4. Then rotate the lid clockwise to lock.
5. Press Power button to turn on the unit.
6. Then press Milkshake button.
7. When the program is completed, turn the Outer Bowl and release it from the machine.
8. Transfer the shake into serving glasses and serve immediately.

Nutrition Info:
- InfoCalories: 210,Fat: 4.9g,Carbohydrates: 36.3g,Protein: 5.4.

Sugar Cookie Milkshake

Servings: 1 | Cooking Time:x

Ingredients:
- ½ C. vanilla ice cream
- ½ C. oat milk
- 3 small sugar cookies, crushed
- 2 tbsp. sprinkles

Directions:
1. In an empty Ninja CREAMi pint container, place the ice cream.
2. With a spoon, create a 1½-inch wide hole in the center that reaches the bottom of the pint container.
3. Add the remaining ingredients into the hole.
4. Arrange the container into the outer bowl of Ninja CREAMi.
5. Install the "Creamerizer Paddle" onto the lid of outer bowl.
6. Then rotate the lid clockwise to lock.
7. Press "Power" button to turn on the unit.
8. Then press "MILKSHAKE" button.
9. When the program is completed, turn the outer bowl and release it from the machine.
10. Transfer the shake into a serving glass and serve immediately.

Nutrition Info:
- InfoCalories: 283,Carbohydrates: 57.8g,Protein: 5.6g,Fat: 5.1g,Sodium: 260m.

Marshmallow Milkshake

Servings: 2 | Cooking Time:x

Ingredients:
- 1½ cups vanilla ice cream
- ½ cup oat milk
- ½ cup marshmallow cereal

Directions:
1. In an empty Ninja CREAMi pint container, place ice cream followed by oat milk and marshmallow cereal.
2. Arrange the container into the Outer Bowl of Ninja CREAMi.
3. Install the Creamerizer Paddle onto the lid of Outer Bowl.
4. Then rotate the lid clockwise to lock.
5. Press Power button to turn on the unit.
6. Then press Milkshake button.
7. When the program is completed, turn the Outer Bowl and release it from the machine.
8. Transfer the shake into serving glasses and serve immediately.

Nutrition Info:
- InfoCalories: 165,Fat: 6.1g,Carbohydrates: 24.8g,Protein: 3.

Cashew Butter Milkshake

Servings: 2 | Cooking Time:x

Ingredients:
- 1½ cups vanilla ice cream
- ½ cup canned cashew milk
- ¼ cup cashew butter

Directions:
1. In an empty Ninja CREAMi pint container, place the ice cream.
2. With a spoon, create a 1½-inch wide hole in the center that reaches the bottom of the pint container.
3. Add the remaining ingredients into the hole.
4. Arrange the container into the Outer Bowl of Ninja CREAMi.
5. Install the Creamerizer Paddle onto the lid of Outer Bowl.
6. Then rotate the lid clockwise to lock.
7. Press Power button to turn on the unit.
8. Then press Milkshake button.
9. When the program is completed, turn the Outer Bowl and release it from the machine.
10. Transfer the shake into serving glasses and serve immediately.

Nutrition Info:
- InfoCalories: 297,Fat: 21.6g,Carbohydrates: 21.1g,Protein: 7.4.

Servings: 2 | Cooking Time:x

Ingredients:
- 1 C. whole milk
- ½ C. amaretto-flavored coffee creamer
- ¼ C. amaretto liqueur
- 1 tbsp. agave nectar
- ¼ C. chocolate chip cookies, chopped

Directions:
1. In an empty Ninja CREAMi pint container, place all ingredients except for cookies and stir to combine.
2. Cover the container with the storage lid and freeze for 24 hours.
3. After 24 hours, remove the lid from container and arrange into the outer bowl of Ninja CREAMi.
4. Install the "Creamerizer Paddle" onto the lid of outer bowl.
5. Then rotate the lid clockwise to lock.
6. Press "Power" button to turn on the unit.
7. Then press "MILKSHAKE" button.
8. When the program is completed, with a spoon, create a 1½-inch wide hole in the center that reaches the bottom of the pint container.
9. Add the chopped cookies into the hole and press "MIX-IN" button.
10. When the program is completed, turn the outer bowl and release it from the machine.
11. Transfer the shake into serving glasses and serve immediately.

Nutrition Info:
- InfoCalories: 371,Carbohydrates: 25.9g,Protein: 6.5g,Fat: 17.6g,Sodium: 294m.

Lite Coffee Chip Ice Cream

Servings:4 | Cooking Time:x

Ingredients:
- ¾ cup unsweetened coconut cream
- ¼ cup monk fruit sweetener with erythritol
- ½ teaspoon stevia sweetener
- 1½ tablespoons instant coffee granules
- 1 cup unsweetened rice milk
- 1 teaspoon vanilla extract
- ¼ cup low-sugar vegan chocolate chips

Directions:
1. In a large bowl, whisk the coconut cream until smooth. Add the monk fruit sweetener, stevia, instant coffee, rice milk, and vanilla to the bowl; whisk until everything is well combined and the sugar is dissolved.
2. Pour the base into a clean CREAMi Pint. Place the storage lid on the container and freeze for 24 hours.
3. Remove the pint from the freezer and take off the lid. Place the pint in the outer bowl of your Ninja CREAMi, install the Creamerizer Paddle in the outer bowl lid, and lock the lid assembly onto the outer bowl. Place the bowl assembly on the motor base, and twist the handle to the right to raise the platform and lock it in place. Select the Lite Ice Cream function.
4. Use a spoon to create a 1½-inch-wide hole that goes all the way to the bottom of the pint. Pour the chocolate chips into the hole. then replace the pint lid and select the Mix-In function.
5. Once the machine has finished processing, remove the ice cream from the pint. Serve immediately.

Avocado Milkshake

Ingredients:

- 1 C. coconut ice cream
- 1 small ripe avocado, peeled, pitted and chopped
- 1 tsp. fresh lemon juice
- 2 tbsp. agave nectar
- 1 tsp. vanilla extract
- Pinch of salt
- ½ C. oat milk

Directions:

1. In an empty Ninja CREAMi pint container, place ice cream, followed by remaining ingredients.
2. Arrange the container into the outer bowl of Ninja CREAMi.
3. Install the "Creamerizer Paddle" onto the lid of outer bowl.
4. Then rotate the lid clockwise to lock.
5. Press "Power" button to turn on the unit.
6. Then press "MILKSHAKE" button.
7. When the program is completed, turn the outer bowl and release it from the machine.
8. Transfer the shake into serving glasses and serve immediately.

Nutrition Info:

- InfoCalories: 283,Carbohydrates: 35.2g,Protein: 3.3g,Fat: 15.2g,Sodium: 134m.

Ice Cream Mix-ins Recipes

Ice Cream Mix-ins Recipes

Jelly & Peanut Butter Ice Cream

Servings: 4 | Cooking Time: 5 Minutes

Ingredients:

- 3 tablespoons granulated sugar
- 4 large egg yolks
- 1 cup whole milk
- ⅓ cup heavy cream
- ¼ cup smooth peanut butter
- 3 tablespoons grape jelly
- ¼ cup honey roasted peanuts, chopped

Directions:

1. 1n a small saucepan, add the sugar and egg yolks and beat until sugar is dissolved.
2. Add the milk, heavy cream, peanut butter, and grape jelly to the saucepan and stir to combine.
3. Place saucepan over medium heat and cook until temperature reaches cook until temperature reaches to 165 -175° F, stirring continuously with a rubber spatula.
4. Remove from the heat and through a fine-mesh strainer, strain the mixture into an empty Ninja CREAMi pint container.
5. Place the container into ice bath to cool.
6. After cooling, cover the container with storage lid and freeze for 24 hours.
7. After 24 hours, remove the lid from container and arrange into the Outer Bowl of Ninja CREAMi.
8. Install the Creamerizer Paddle onto the lid of Outer Bowl.
9. Then rotate the lid clockwise to lock.
10. Press Power button to turn on the unit.
11. Then press ICE CREAM button.
12. When the program is completed, with a spoon, create a 1½-inch wide hole in the center that reaches the bottom of the pint container.
13. Add the peanuts into the hole and press Mix-In button.
14. When the program is completed, turn the Outer Bowl and release it from the machine.
15. Transfer the ice cream into serving bowls and serve immediately.

Nutrition Info:

- InfoCalories: 349,Fat: 23.1g,Carbohydrates: 27.5g,Protein: 11.5.

Coconut Mint Chip Ice Cream

Servings:4 | Cooking Time:x

Ingredients:

- 1 can full-fat unsweetened coconut milk
- ½ cup organic sugar
- ½ teaspoon mint extract
- ¼ cup mini vegan chocolate chips

Directions:

1. In a medium bowl, whisk together the coconut milk, sugar, and mint extract until everything is well combined and the sugar is dissolved.
2. Pour the base into a clean CREAMi Pint. Place the storage lid on the container and freeze for 24 hours.
3. Remove the pint from the freezer and take off the lid. Place the pint in the outer bowl of your Ninja CREAMi, install the Creamerizer Paddle in the outer bowl lid, and lock the lid assembly onto the outer bowl. Place the bowl assembly on the motor base, and twist the handle to the right to raise the platform and lock it in place. Select the Ice Cream function.
4. Once the machine has finished processing, remove the lid from the pint container. With a spoon, create a 1½-inch-wide hole that reaches the bottom of the pint. During this process, it is okay if your treat reaches above the Max Fill line. Add the mini chocolate chips to the hole in the pint, replace the lid, and select the Mix-In function.
5. Once the machine has finished processing, remove the ice cream from the pint. Serve immediately with desired toppings.

Lite Chocolate Cookie Ice Cream

Servings: 2 | Cooking Time: 24 Hours And 5 Minutes

Ingredients:
- 1 tablespoon cream cheese, at room temperature
- 2 tablespoons unsweetened cocoa powder
- ½ teaspoon stevia sweetener
- 3 tablespoons raw agave nectar
- 1 teaspoon vanilla extract
- ¾ cup heavy cream
- 1 cup whole milk
- ¼ cup crushed reduced-fat sugar cookies

Directions:
1. Place the cream cheese in a large microwave-safe bowl and heat on high for 10 seconds.
2. Mix in the cocoa powder, stevia, agave, and vanilla. Microwave for 60 seconds more, or until the mixture resembles frosting.
3. Slowly whisk in the heavy cream and milk until the sugar has dissolved and the mixture is thoroughly mixed.
4. Pour the base into a clean CREAMi Pint. Place the storage lid on the container and freeze for 24 hours.
5. Remove the Pint from the freezer and take off the lid. Place the Pint in the outer bowl of your Ninja CREAMi, install the Creamerizer Paddle in the outer bowl lid, and lock the lid assembly onto the outer bowl. Place the bowl assembly on the motor base, and twist the handle to the right to raise the platform and lock it in place. Select the LITE ICE CREAM function.
6. Once the machine has finished processing, remove the lid. With a spoon, create a 1½-inch-wide hole that reaches the bottom of the Pint. During this process, it's okay if your treat goes above the max fill line. Add the crushed cookies to the hole in the Pint. Replace the Pint lid and select the MIX-IN function.
7. Once the machine has finished processing, remove the ice cream from the Pint.

Nutrition Info:
- InfoCalories 150,Protein 5g,Carbohydrate 25g,Fat 4g,Sodium 65mg.

Mint Chocolate Chip Ice Cream

Servings: 4 | Cooking Time: 24 Hours And 5 Minutes

Ingredients:
- 1 tablespoon cream cheese, softened
- ⅓ cup granulated sugar
- 1 teaspoon vanilla extract
- ¾ cup heavy cream
- 1 cup whole milk
- 1 teaspoon mint extract
- Green food coloring (optional)
- ¼ cup mini chocolate chips, for mix-in

Directions:
1. Microwave the cream cheese for 10 seconds in a large microwave-safe bowl. Combine with the sugar and mint extract in a mixing bowl using a whisk or rubber spatula for about 60 seconds or until the mixture resembles frosting.
2. Slowly whisk in the heavy cream, milk, and optional food coloring until thoroughly mixed and the sugar has dissolved.
3. Pour the base into an empty CREAMi Pint. Place the storage lid on the Pint and freeze for 24 hours.
4. Remove the Pint from the freezer and remove its lid. Place the Pint in the outer bowl, install the Creamerizer Paddle onto the outer bowl lid, and lock the lid assembly on the outer bowl. Place the bowl assembly on the motor base, twist the handle to raise the platform, and lock it in place.
5. Select ICE CREAM.
6. With a spoon, create a 1½-inch wide hole that reaches the bottom of the Pint. During this process, it's okay for your treat to press above the max fill line. Add the chocolate chips to the hole and process again using the MIX-IN program.
7. When processing is complete, remove the ice cream from the Pint.

Nutrition Info:
- InfoCalories 170,Protein 2g,Carbohydrate 18g,Fat 8g,Sodium 45mg.

Chocolate Brownie Ice Cream

Ingredients:
- 1 tablespoon cream cheese, softened
- ⅓ cup granulated sugar
- 1 teaspoon vanilla extract
- 2 tablespoons cocoa powder
- 1 cup whole milk
- ¾ cup heavy cream
- 2 tablespoons mini chocolate chips
- 2 tablespoons brownie chunks

Directions:
1. 1n a large microwave-safe bowl, add the cream cheese and microwave on High for about ten seconds.
2. Remove from the microwave and stir until smooth.
3. Add the sugar and almond extract and with a wire whisk, beat until the mixture looks like frosting.
4. Slowly add the milk and heavy cream and beat until well combined.
5. Transfer the mixture into an empty Ninja CREAMi pint container.
6. Cover the container with storage lid and freeze for 24 hours.
7. After 24 hours, remove the lid from container and arrange into the Outer Bowl of Ninja CREAMi.
8. Install the Creamerizer Paddle onto the lid of Outer Bowl.
9. Then rotate the lid clockwise to lock.
10. Press Power button to turn on the unit.
11. Then press Ice Cream button.
12. When the program is completed, with a spoon, create a 1½-inch wide hole in the center that reaches the bottom of the pint container.
13. Add the chocolate chunks and brownie pieces into the hole and press Mix-In button.
14. When the program is completed, turn the Outer Bowl and release it from the machine.
15. Transfer the ice cream into serving bowls and serve immediately.

Nutrition Info:
- InfoCalories: 232,Fat: 13.7g,Carbohydrates: 25.9g,Protein: 3.6.

Coffee And Cookies Ice Cream

Ingredients:
- 1 tablespoon cream cheese, at room temperature
- ⅓ cup granulated sugar
- 1 teaspoon vanilla extract
- 1 tablespoon instant espresso
- ¾ cup heavy (whipping) cream
- 1 cup whole milk
- ¼ cup crushed chocolate sandwich cookies

Directions:
1. In a large bowl, whisk together the cream cheese, sugar, and vanilla for about 1 minute, until the mixture looks like frosting.
2. Slowly whisk in the instant espresso, heavy cream, and milk until fully combined.
3. Pour the base into a clean CREAMi Pint. Place the lid on the container and freeze for 24 hours.
4. Remove the pint from the freezer and take off the lid. Place the pint in the outer bowl of your Ninja CREAMi, install the Creamerizer Paddle in the outer bowl lid, and lock the lid assembly onto the outer bowl. Place the bowl assembly on the motor base, and twist the handle to the right to raise the platform and lock it in place. Select the Ice Cream function.
5. Once the machine has finished processing, remove the lid from the pint container. With a spoon, create a 1½-inch-wide hole that reaches the bottom of the pint. Add the crushed cookies to the hole, replace the lid, and select the Mix-In function.
6. Once the machine has finished processing, remove the ice cream from the pint. Serve immediately.

Triple-chocolate Ice Cream

Servings:4 | Cooking Time:x

Ingredients:
- 4 large egg yolks
- ⅓ cup granulated sugar
- 1 tablespoon unsweetened cocoa powder
- 1 tablespoon hot fudge sauce
- ¾ cup heavy (whipping) cream
- ½ cup whole milk
- 1 teaspoon vanilla extract
- ¼ cup white chocolate chips

Directions:
1. Fill a large bowl with ice water and set it aside.
2. In a small saucepan, whisk together the egg yolks, sugar, and cocoa powder until the mixture is fully combined and the sugar is dissolved. Do not do this over heat.
3. Whisk in the hot fudge, heavy cream, milk, and vanilla.
4. Place the pan over medium heat. Cook, stirring constantly with a rubber spatula, until the temperature reaches 165°F to 175°F on an instant-read thermometer.
5. Remove the pan from the heat and pour the base through a fine-mesh strainer into a clean CREAMi Pint. Carefully place the container in the prepared ice water bath, making sure the water doesn't spill into the base.
6. Once the base has cooled, place the storage lid on the pint and freeze for 24 hours.
7. Remove the pint from the freezer and take off the lid. Place the pint in the outer bowl of your Ninja CREAMi, install the Creamerizer Paddle in the outer bowl lid, and lock the lid assembly onto the outer bowl. Place the bowl assembly on the motor base, and twist the handle to the right to raise the platform and lock it in place. Select the Ice Cream function.
8. Once the machine has finished processing, remove the lid from the pint container. With a spoon, create a 1½-inch-wide hole that reaches the bottom of the pint. During this process, it is okay if your treat reaches above the Max Fill line. Add the white chocolate chips to the hole in the pint, replace the lid, and select the Mix-In function.
9. Once the machine has finished processing, remove the ice cream from the pint. Serve immediately with desired toppings.

Mint Cookies Ice Cream

Servings: 4 | Cooking Time:x

Ingredients:
- ¾ cup coconut cream
- ¼ cup monk fruit sweetener with Erythritol
- 2 tablespoons agave nectar
- ½ teaspoon mint extract
- 5-6 drops green food coloring
- 1 cup oat milk
- 3 chocolate sandwich cookies, quartered

Directions:
1. 1n a large bowl, add the coconut cream and beat until smooth.
2. Add the sweetener, agave nectar, mint extract and food coloring and beat until sweetener is dissolved.
3. Add the oat milk and beat until well combined.
4. Transfer the mixture into an empty Ninja CREAMi pint container.
5. Cover the container with storage lid and freeze for 24 hours.
6. After 24 hours, remove the lid from container and arrange into the Outer Bowl of Ninja CREAMi.
7. Install the Creamerizer Paddle onto the lid of Outer Bowl.
8. Then rotate the lid clockwise to lock.
9. Press Power button to turn on the unit.
10. Then press Lite Ice Cream button.
11. When the program is completed, with a spoon, create a 1½-inch wide hole in the center that reaches the bottom of the pint container.
12. Add the cookie pieces into the hole and press Mix-In button.
13. When the program is completed, turn the Outer Bowl and release it from the machine.
14. Transfer the ice cream into serving bowls and serve immediately.

Nutrition Info:
- InfoCalories: 201,Fat: 12.8g,Carbohydrates: 21.9g,Protein: 2.4.

Sweet Potato Pie Ice Cream

Servings:4 | Cooking Time:x

Ingredients:
- 1 cup canned pureed sweet potato
- 1 tablespoon corn syrup
- ¼ cup plus 1 tablespoon light brown sugar
- 1 teaspoon vanilla extract
- 1 teaspoon cinnamon
- ¾ cup heavy (whipping) cream
- ¼ cup mini marshmallows

Directions:
1. Combine the sweet potato puree, corn syrup, brown sugar, vanilla, and cinnamon in a blender. Blend on high until smooth.
2. Pour the base into a clean CREAMi Pint. Whisk in the heavy cream until combined. Place the storage lid on the container and freeze for 24 hours.
3. Remove the pint from the freezer and take off the lid. Place the pint in the outer bowl of your Ninja CREAMi, install the Creamerizer Paddle in the outer bowl lid, and lock the lid assembly onto the outer bowl. Place the bowl assembly on the motor base, and twist the handle to the right to raise the platform and lock it in place. Select the Ice Cream function.
4. Once the machine has finished processing, remove the lid from the pint container. With a spoon, create a 1½-inch-wide hole that reaches the bottom of the pint. During this process, it is okay if your treat reaches above the Max Fill line. Add the marshmallows to the hole in the pint, replace the lid, and select the Mix-In function.
5. Once the machine has finished processing, remove the ice cream from the pint. Serve immediately with desired toppings.

Lavender Cookie Ice Cream

Servings: 4 | Cooking Time: 10 Minutes

Ingredients:
- ¾ cup heavy cream
- 1 tablespoon dried culinary lavender
- 1/8 teaspoon salt
- ¾ cup whole milk
- ½ cup sweetened condensed milk
- 4 drops purple food coloring
- ⅓ cup chocolate wafer cookies, crushed

Directions:
1. In a medium saucepan, add heavy cream, lavender and salt and mix well.
2. Place the saucepan over low heat and steep, covered for about ten minutes, stirring after every two minutes.
3. Remove from the heat and through a fine-mesh strainer, strain the cream mixture into a large bowl.
4. Discard the lavender leaves.
5. In the bowl of cream mixture, add the milk, condensed milk and purple food coloring and beat until smooth.
6. Transfer the mixture into an empty Ninja CREAMi pint container.
7. Cover the container with storage lid and freeze for 24 hours.
8. After 24 hours, remove the lid from container and arrange into the Outer Bowl of Ninja CREAMi.
9. Install the Creamerizer Paddle onto the lid of Outer Bowl.
10. Then rotate the lid clockwise to lock.
11. Press Power button to turn on the unit.
12. Then press Ice Cream button.
13. When the program is completed, with a spoon, create a 1½-inch wide hole in the center that reaches the bottom of the pint container.
14. Add the crushed cookies the hole and press Mix-In button.
15. When the program is completed, turn the Outer Bowl and release it from the machine.
16. Transfer the ice cream into serving bowls and serve immediately.

Nutrition Info:
- InfoCalories: 229,Fat: 13.2g,Carbohydrates: 23.5g,Protein: 5.

Chocolate-covered Coconut And Almond Ice Cream

Servings:4 | Cooking Time:x

Ingredients:
- DAIRY-FREE, EGG-FREE, VEGAN
- PREP TIME: 5 minutes / Freeze time: 24 hours
- Functions: Ice Cream, Mix-In
- TOOLS NEEDED: Medium bowl, whisk, spoon
- 1 can full-fat unsweetened coconut milk
- ¼ cup unsweetened almond milk
- ½ cup organic sugar
- 1 teaspoon vanilla extract
- 2 tablespoons toasted almond halves
- 2 tablespoons vegan chocolate chips

Directions:
1. In a medium bowl, whisk together the coconut milk, almond milk, sugar, and vanilla until everything is incorporated and the sugar is dissolved.
2. Pour the base into a clean CREAMi Pint. Place the storage lid on the container and freeze for 24 hours.
3. Remove the pint from the freezer and take off the lid. Place the pint in the outer bowl of your Ninja CREAMi, install the Creamerizer Paddle in the outer bowl lid, and lock the lid assembly onto the outer bowl. Place the bowl assembly on the motor base, and twist the handle to the right to raise the platform and lock it in place. Select the Ice Cream function.
4. Once the machine has finished processing, remove the lid from the pint container. With a spoon, create a 1½-inch-wide hole that reaches the bottom of the pint. Add the almond halves and chocolate chips to the hole, then replace the lid and select the Mix-In function.
5. Once the machine has finished processing, remove the ice cream from the pint. Serve immediately.

Pistachio Ice Cream

Servings: 4 | Cooking Time:x

Ingredients:
- 1 tablespoon cream cheese, softened
- ⅓ cup granulated sugar
- 1 teaspoon almond extract
- 1 cup whole milk
- ¾ cup heavy cream
- ¼ cup pistachios, shells removed and chopped

Directions:
1. In a large microwave-safe bowl, add the cream cheese and microwave on High for about ten seconds.
2. Remove from the microwave and stir until smooth.
3. Add the sugar and almond extract and with a wire whisk, beat until the mixture looks like frosting.
4. Slowly add the milk and heavy cream and beat until well combined.
5. Transfer the mixture into an empty Ninja CREAMi pint container.
6. Cover the container with storage lid and freeze for 24 hours.
7. After 24 hours, remove the lid from container and arrange into the Outer Bowl of Ninja CREAMi.
8. Install the Creamerizer Paddle onto the lid of Outer Bowl.
9. Then rotate the lid clockwise to lock.
10. Press Power button to turn on the unit.
11. Then press Ice Cream button.
12. When the program is completed, with a spoon, create a 1½-inch wide hole in the center that reaches the bottom of the pint container.
13. Add the pistachios into the hole and press Mix-In button.
14. When the program is completed, turn the Outer Bowl and release it from the machine.
15. Transfer the ice cream into serving bowls and serve immediately.

Nutrition Info:
- InfoCalories: 208,Fat: 12.9g,Carbohydrates: 21.3g,Protein: 3.4.

Bourbon-maple-walnut Ice Cream

Ingredients:
- 4 large egg yolks
- ¼ cup maple syrup
- ¼ cup corn syrup
- 2 tablespoons bourbon
- ½ cup whole milk
- 1 cup heavy (whipping) cream
- ¼ cup toasted walnut halves

Directions:
1. Fill a large bowl with ice water and set it aside.
2. In a small saucepan, whisk together the egg yolks, maple syrup, corn syrup, and bourbon until the mixture is fully combined. Do not do this over heat.
3. Whisk in the milk and heavy cream.
4. Place the pan over medium heat. Cook, stirring constantly with a rubber spatula, until the temperature reaches 165°F to 175°F on an instant-read thermometer.
5. Remove the pan from the heat and pour the base into a clean CREAMi Pint. Carefully place the container in the prepared ice water bath, making sure the water doesn't spill into the base.
6. Once the base has cooled, place the storage lid on the pint and freeze for 24 hours.
7. Remove the pint from the freezer and take off the lid. Place the pint in the outer bowl of your Ninja CREAMi, install the Creamerizer Paddle in the outer bowl lid, and lock the lid assembly onto the outer bowl. Place the bowl assembly on the motor base, and twist the handle to the right to raise the platform and lock it in place. Select the Ice Cream function.
8. Once the machine has finished processing, remove the lid from the pint container. With a spoon, create a 1½-inch-wide hole that reaches the bottom of the pint. During this process, it is okay if your treat reaches above the Max Fill line. Add the toasted walnuts to the hole in the pint, replace the lid, and select the Mix-In function.
9. Once the machine has finished processing, remove the ice cream from the pint. Serve immediately.

Cookies & Cream Ice Cream

Ingredients:
- ½ tablespoon cream cheese, softened
- ¼ cup granulated sugar
- ½ teaspoon vanilla extract
- ½ cup heavy cream
- ½ cup whole milk
- 1½ chocolate sandwich cookies, broken, for mix-in

Directions:
1. Microwave the cream cheese for 10 seconds in a large microwave-safe bowl. Combine the sugar and vanilla extract in a mixing bowl and whisk or scrape together until the mixture resembles frosting, about 60 seconds.
2. Slowly whisk in the heavy cream and milk until smooth and the sugar has dissolved.
3. Pour the base into an empty CREAMi Pint. Place storage lid on the Pint and freeze for 24 hours.
4. Remove the Pint from the freezer and remove the lid from the Pint. Place the Pint in the outer bowl, install Creamerizer Paddle onto the outer bowl lid, and lock the lid assembly on the outer bowl. Select ICE CREAM.
5. With a spoon, create a 1½-inch wide hole that reaches the bottom of the Pint. During this process, it's okay for your treat to go above the max fill line. Add the broken chocolate sandwich cookies to the hole and process again using the MIX-IN program.
6. When processing is complete, remove the ice cream from the Pint and serve immediately.

Nutrition Info:
- InfoCalories 140,Protein 2g,Carbohydrate 23g,Fat 4g,Sodium 86mg.

Grasshopper Ice Cream

Servings: 4 | Cooking Time:x

Ingredients:

- ½ cup frozen spinach, thawed and squeezed dry
- 1 cup whole milk
- ½ cup granulated sugar
- 1 teaspoon mint extract
- 3-5 drops green food coloring
- ⅓ cup heavy cream
- ¼ cup chocolate chunks, chopped
- ¼ cup brownie, cut into 1-inch pieces

Directions:

1. In a high-speed blender, add the spinach, milk, sugar, mint extract and food coloring and pulse until mixture smooth.
2. Transfer the mixture into an empty Ninja CREAMi pint container.
3. Add the heavy cream and stir until well combined.
4. Cover the container with storage lid and freeze for 24 hours.
5. After 24 hours, remove the lid from container and arrange into the Outer Bowl of Ninja CREAMi.
6. Install the Creamerizer Paddle onto the lid of Outer Bowl.
7. Then rotate the lid clockwise to lock.
8. Press Power button to turn on the unit.
9. Then press Ice Cream button.
10. When the program is completed, with a spoon, create a 1½-inch wide hole in the center that reaches the bottom of the pint container.
11. Add the chocolate chunks and brownie pieces into the hole and press Mix-In button.
12. When the program is completed, turn the Outer Bowl and release it from the machine.
13. Transfer the ice cream into serving bowls and serve immediately.

Nutrition Info:

- InfoCalories: 243,Fat: 10.1g,Carbohydrates: 36.7g,Protein: 3.4.

Rum Raisin Ice Cream

Servings: 4 | Cooking Time: 24 Hours And 23 Minutes

Ingredients:

- 3 large egg yolks
- ¼ cup dark brown sugar (or coconut sugar)
- 1 tablespoon light corn syrup
- ½ cup heavy cream
- 1 cup whole milk
- 1 teaspoon rum extract
- ⅓ cup raisins
- ¼ cup dark or spiced rum

Directions:

1. In a small saucepan, combine the egg yolks, sugar, and corn syrup. Whisk until everything is well mixed and the sugar has dissolved. Whisk together the heavy cream and milk until smooth.
2. Stir the mixture frequently with a whisk or a rubber spatula in a saucepan over medium-low heat. Using an instant-read thermometer, cook until the temperature hits 165°F–175°F.
3. Remove the base from heat, stir in the rum extract, then pour through a fine-mesh strainer into an empty CREAMi Pint. Place into an ice bath. Once cooled, place the storage lid on the Pint and freeze for 24 hours.
4. While the base is cooling, prepare the mix-in. Add the raisins and rum to a small bowl and microwave for 1 minute. Let cool, then drain the remaining rum. Cover and set aside.
5. Remove the Pint from the freezer and remove its lid. Place the Pint in the outer bowl, install the Creamerizer Paddle onto the outer bowl lid, and lock the lid assembly on the outer bowl. Select ICE CREAM.
6. With a spoon, create a 1½-inch wide hole that reaches the bottom of the Pint. Add the mixed raisins to the hole and process again using the MIX-IN program.
7. When processing is complete, remove the ice cream from the Pint.

Nutrition Info:

- InfoCalories 160,Protein 2g,Carbohydrate 18g,Fat 7g,Sodium 45mg.

Sneaky Mint Chip Ice Cream

Servings:4 | Cooking Time:x

Ingredients:

- 3 large egg yolks
- 1 tablespoon corn syrup
- ¼ cup granulated sugar
- ⅓ cup whole milk
- ¾ cup heavy (whipping) cream
- 1 cup packed fresh spinach
- ½ cup frozen peas, thawed
- 1 teaspoon mint extract
- ¼ cup semisweet chocolate chips

Directions:

1. Fill a large bowl with ice water and set it aside.
2. In a small saucepan, whisk together the egg yolks, corn syrup, and sugar until the mixture is fully combined and the sugar is dissolved. Do not do this over heat.
3. Whisk in the milk and heavy cream.
4. Place the pan over medium heat. Cook, stirring constantly with a rubber spatula, until the temperature reaches 165°F to 175°F on an instant-read thermometer.
5. Remove the pan from the heat and pour the base into a clean CREAMi Pint. Carefully place the container in the prepared ice water bath, making sure the water doesn't spill into the base.
6. Once the mixture has completely cooled, pour the base into a blender and add the spinach, peas, and mint extract. Blend on high for 30 seconds. Strain the base through a fine-mesh strainer back into the CREAMi Pint. Place the storage lid on the container and freeze for 24 hours.
7. Remove the pint from the freezer and take off the lid. Place the pint in the outer bowl of your Ninja CREAMi, install the Creamerizer Paddle in the outer bowl lid, and lock the lid assembly onto the outer bowl. Place the bowl assembly on the motor base, and twist the handle to the right to raise the platform and lock it in place. Select the Ice Cream function.
8. Once the machine has finished processing, remove the lid from the pint container. With a spoon, create a 1½-inch-wide hole that reaches the bottom of the pint. During this process, it is okay if your treat reaches above the Max Fill line. Add the chocolate chips to the hole in the pint, replace the lid, and select the Mix-In function.
9. Once the machine has finished processing, remove the ice cream from the pint. Serve immediately.

Lavender Cookies & Cream Ice Cream

Servings: 2 | Cooking Time: 24 Hours And 20 Minutes

Ingredients:

- ½ cup heavy cream
- ½ tablespoon dried culinary lavender
- ¼ teaspoon kosher salt
- ½ cup whole milk
- ¼ cup sweetened condensed milk
- 2 drops purple food coloring
- ¼ cup crushed chocolate wafer cookies

Directions:

1. Whisk together the heavy cream, lavender, and salt in a medium saucepan.
2. Steep the mixture for 10 minutes over low heat, stirring every 2 minutes to prevent bubbling.
3. Using a fine-mesh strainer, drain the lavender from the heavy cream into a large mixing basin. Discard the lavender.
4. Combine the milk, sweetened condensed milk, and purple food coloring in a large mixing bowl. Whisk until the mixture is completely smooth.
5. Pour the base into an empty CREAMi Pint. Place the Pint into an ice bath. Once cooled, place the storage lid on the Pint and freeze for 24 hours.
6. Remove the Pint from the freezer and remove its lid. Place Pint in outer bowl, install Creamerizer Paddle in outer bowl lid, and lock the lid assembly onto the outer bowl. Select ICE CREAM.
7. When the process is done, create a 1½-inch wide hole that reaches the bottom of the Pint with a spoon. It's okay if your treat exceeds the max fill line. Add crushed wafer cookies to the hole and process again using the MIX-IN program.
8. When processing is complete, remove ice cream from Pint and serve immediately, topped with extra crumbled wafers if desired.

Nutrition Info:

- InfoCalories 180,Protein 3g,Carbohydrate 19g,Fat 16g,Sodium 60mg.

Snack Mix Ice Cream

Servings: 4 | Cooking Time: 10 Seconds

Ingredients:
- 1 tablespoon cream cheese, softened
- ⅓ cup granulated sugar
- ½ teaspoon vanilla extract
- 1 cup whole milk
- ¾ cup heavy cream
- 2 tablespoons sugar cone pieces
- 1 tablespoon mini pretzels
- 1 tablespoon potato chips, crushed

Directions:
1. In a large microwave-safe bowl, add the cream cheese and microwave on High for about ten seconds.
2. Remove from the microwave and stir until smooth.
3. Add the sugar and vanilla extract and with a wire whisk, beat until the mixture looks like frosting.
4. Slowly add the milk and heavy cream and beat until well combined.
5. Transfer the mixture into an empty Ninja CREAMi pint container.
6. Cover the container with storage lid and freeze for 24 hours.
7. After 24 hours, remove the lid from container and arrange into the Outer Bowl of Ninja CREAMi.
8. Install the Creamerizer Paddle onto the lid of Outer Bowl.
9. Then rotate the lid clockwise to lock.
10. Press Power button to turn on the unit.
11. Then press Ice Cream button.
12. When the program is completed, with a spoon, create a 1½-inch wide hole in the center that reaches the bottom of the pint container.
13. Add the cone pieces, pretzels and potato chips into the hole and press Mix-In button.
14. When the program is completed, turn the Outer Bowl and release it from the machine.
15. Transfer the ice cream into serving bowls and serve immediately.

Nutrition Info:
- InfoCalories: 182,Fat: 4.3g,Carbohydrates: 32.8g,Protein: 3.6.

Coffee Chip Ice Cream

Servings: 4 | Cooking Time:x

Ingredients:
- ¾ cup heavy cream
- ¼ cup monk fruit sweetener with Erythritol
- ½ teaspoon stevia sweetener
- 1½ tablespoons instant coffee granules
- 1 cup unsweetened almond milk
- 1 teaspoon vanilla extract
- 3 tablespoons chocolate chips
- 1 tablespoon walnuts, chopped

Directions:
1. In a bowl, add the heavy cream and beat until smooth.
2. Add the remaining ingredients except for chocolate chips and walnuts and beat sweetener is dissolved.
3. Transfer the mixture into an empty Ninja CREAMi pint container.
4. Cover the container with storage lid and freeze for 24 hours.
5. After 24 hours, remove the lid from container and arrange into the Outer Bowl of Ninja CREAMi.
6. Install the Creamerizer Paddle onto the lid of Outer Bowl.
7. Then rotate the lid clockwise to lock.
8. Press Power button to turn on the unit.
9. Then press Lite Ice Cream button.
10. When the program is completed, with a spoon, create a 1½-inch wide hole in the center that reaches the bottom of the pint container.
11. Add the chocolate chips and walnuts into the hole and press Mix-In button.
12. When the program is completed, turn the Outer Bowl and release it from the machine.
13. Transfer the ice cream into serving bowls and serve immediately.

Nutrition Info:
- InfoCalories: 145,Fat: 12.7g,Carbohydrates: 6.1g,Protein: 1.8.

Servings:4 | Cooking Time:x

Ingredients:

- 5 large egg yolks
- ¼ cup corn syrup
- 2½ tablespoons granulated sugar
- ⅓ cup whole milk
- 1 cup heavy (whipping) cream
- 1½ tablespoons vanilla extract
- 3 tablespoons vanilla cake mix
- 2 tablespoons rainbow-colored sprinkles

Directions:

1. Fill a large bowl with ice water and set it aside.
2. In a small saucepan, whisk together the egg yolks, corn syrup, and sugar until the mixture is fully combined and the sugar is dissolved. Do not do this over heat.
3. Whisk in the milk, heavy cream, and vanilla.
4. Place the pan over medium heat. Cook, stirring constantly with a rubber spatula, until the temperature reaches 165°F to 175°F on an instant-read thermometer.
5. Remove the pan from the heat and pour the base through a fine-mesh strainer into a clean CREAMi Pint. Carefully place the container in the prepared ice water bath, making sure the water doesn't spill into the base.
6. Once the base has cooled, whisk in the vanilla cake mix until it is fully incorporated. Place the storage lid on the pint container and freeze for 24 hours.
7. Remove the pint from the freezer and take off the lid. Place the pint in the outer bowl of your Ninja CREAMi, install the Creamerizer Paddle in the outer bowl lid, and lock the lid assembly onto the outer bowl. Place the bowl assembly on the motor base, and twist the handle to the right to raise the platform and lock it in place. Select the Ice Cream function.
8. Once the machine has finished processing, remove the lid from the pint container. With a spoon, create a 1½-inch-wide hole that reaches the bottom of the pint. During this process, it is okay if your treat reaches above the Max Fill line. Add the rainbow sprinkles to the hole in the pint, replace the lid, and select the Mix-In function.
9. Once the machine has finished processing, remove the ice cream from the pint. Serve immediately.

Rocky Road Ice Cream

Servings: 4 | Cooking Time:x

Ingredients:
- 1 cup whole milk
- ½ cup frozen cauliflower florets, thawed
- ½ cup dark brown sugar
- 3 tablespoons dark cocoa powder
- 1 teaspoon chocolate extract
- ⅓ cup heavy cream
- 2 tablespoons almonds, sliced
- 2 tablespoons mini marshmallows
- 2 tablespoons mini chocolate chips

Directions:
1. In a high-speed blender, add milk, cauliflower, brown sugar, cocoa powder, and chocolate extract and pulse until smooth.
2. Transfer the mixture into an empty Ninja CREAMi pint container.
3. Add the heavy cream and stir until well combined.
4. Cover the container with storage lid and freeze for 24 hours.
5. After 24 hours, remove the lid from container and arrange into the Outer Bowl of Ninja CREAMi.
6. Install the Creamerizer Paddle onto the lid of Outer Bowl.
7. Then rotate the lid clockwise to lock.
8. Press Power button to turn on the unit.
9. Then press Ice Cream button.
10. When the program is completed, with a spoon, create a 1½-inch wide hole in the center that reaches the bottom of the pint container.
11. Add the almonds, marshmallows and chocolate chips into the hole and press Mix-In button.
12. When the program is completed, turn the Outer Bowl and release it from the machine.
13. Transfer the ice cream into serving bowls and serve immediately.

Nutrition Info:
- InfoCalories: 202,Fat: 9.3g,Carbohydrates: 28.7g,Protein: 4.2.

Fruity Cereal Ice Cream

Servings: 2 | Cooking Time: 24 Hours And 30 Minutes

Ingredients:
- ¾ cup whole milk
- 1 cup fruity cereal, divided
- 1 tablespoon Philadelphia cream cheese, softened
- ¼ cup granulated sugar
- 1 teaspoon vanilla extract
- ½ cup heavy cream

Directions:
1. In a large mixing bowl, combine ½ cup of the fruity cereal and the milk. Allow the mixture to settle for 15–30 minutes, stirring occasionally to infuse the milk with the fruity taste.
2. Microwave the Philadelphia cream cheese for 10 seconds in a second large microwave-safe dish. Combine the sugar and vanilla extract in a mixing bowl with a whisk or rubber spatula until the mixture resembles frosting, about 60 seconds.
3. After 15 to 30 minutes, sift the milk and cereal into the bowl with the sugar mixture using a fine-mesh filter. To release extra milk, press on the cereal with a spoon, then discard it. Mix in the heavy cream until everything is thoroughly mixed.
4. Pour the mixture into an empty ninja CREAMi Pint container. Add the strawberries to the Pint, making sure not to go over the max fill line, and freeze for 24 hours.
5. After 24 hours, remove the Pint from the freezer. Remove the lid.
6. Place the Ninja CREAMi Pint into the outer bowl. Place the outer bowl with the Pint in it into the ninja CREAMi machine and turn until the outer bowl locks into place. Push the ICE CREAM button. During the ICE CREAM function, the ice cream will mix together and become very creamy.
7. Use a spoon to create a 1½-inch wide hole that reaches the bottom of the Pint. Add the remaining ½ cup of fruity cereal to the hole and process again using the mix-in. When processing is complete, remove the ice cream from the Pint.

Nutrition Info:
- InfoCalories 140,Protein 0.5g,Carbohydrate 25g,Fat 2g,Sodium 46mg.

Smoothie Bowls Recipes

Smoothie Bowls Recipes

Papaya Smoothie Bowl

Servings: 2 | Cooking Time:x

Ingredients:
- 2 C. ripe papaya, peeled and cut into 1-inch pieces
- 14 oz. whole milk
- 4-6 drops liquid stevia
- ¼ tsp. vanilla extract

Directions:
1. Place the mango pieces into an empty Ninja CREAMi pint container.
2. Top with coconut milk, stevia and vanilla extract and stir to combine.
3. Cover the container with the storage lid and freeze for 24 hours.
4. After 24 hours, remove the lid from container and arrange into the outer bowl of Ninja CREAMi.
5. Install the "Creamerizer Paddle" onto the lid of outer bowl.
6. Then rotate the lid clockwise to lock.
7. Press "Power" button to turn on the unit.
8. Then press "SMOOTHIE BOWL" button.
9. When the program is completed, turn the outer bowl and release it from the machine.
10. Transfer the smoothie into serving bowls and serve immediately.

Nutrition Info:
- InfoCalories: 183,Carbohydrates: 24.7g,Protein: 7.1g,Fat: 6.9g,Sodium: 91m.

Mango Smoothie Bowl

Servings: 4 | Cooking Time:x

Ingredients:
- 2 cups ripe mango, peeled, pitted and cut into 1-inch pieces
- 1 can of unsweetened coconut milk

Directions:
1. Place the mango pieces into an empty Ninja CREAMi pint container.
2. Top with coconut milk and stir to combine.
3. Cover the container with storage lid and freeze for 24 hours.
4. After 24 hours, remove the lid from container and arrange into the Outer Bowl of Ninja CREAMi.
5. Install the Creamerizer Paddle onto the lid of Outer Bowl.
6. Then rotate the lid clockwise to lock.
7. Press Power button to turn on the unit.
8. Then press Smoothie Bowl button.
9. When the program is completed, turn the Outer Bowl and release it from the machine.
10. Transfer the smoothie into serving bowls and serve immediately.

Nutrition Info:
- InfoCalories: 198,Fat: 14g,Carbohydrates: 14.8g,Protein: 1..

Avocado And Kale Smoothie Bowl

Servings:4 | Cooking Time:x

Ingredients:
- 1 banana, cut into 1-inch pieces
- ½ ripe avocado, cut into 1-inch pieces
- 1 cup packed kale leaves
- 1 cup green apple pieces
- ¼ cup unsweetened coconut milk
- 2 tablespoons agave nectar

Directions:
1. Combine the banana, avocado, kale, apple, coconut milk, and agave in a blender. Blend on high for about 1 minute until smooth.
2. Pour the base into a clean CREAMi Pint. Place the storage lid on the container and freeze for 24 hours.
3. Remove the pint from the freezer and take off the lid. Place the pint in the outer bowl of your Ninja CREAMi, install the Creamerizer Paddle in the outer bowl lid, and lock the lid assembly onto the outer bowl. Place the bowl assembly on the motor base, and twist the handle to the right to raise the platform and lock it in place. Select the Smoothie Bowl function.
4. Once the machine has finished processing, remove the smoothie bowl from the pint. Serve immediately with your desired toppings.

Piescream

Servings:4 | Cooking Time:x

Ingredients:
- 1 can cherry pie filling
- 1 store-bought frozen graham cracker crust
- 1 container whipped topping

Directions:
1. Fill a clean CREAMi Pint to the max fill line with the pie filing. Place the storage lid on the container and freeze for 24 hours.
2. Remove the pint from the freezer and take off the lid. Place the pint in the outer bowl of your Ninja CREAMi, install the Creamerizer Paddle in the outer bowl lid, and lock the lid assembly onto the outer bowl. Place the bowl assembly on the motor base, and twist the handle to the right to raise the platform and lock it in place. Select the Sorbet function.
3. Once the machine has finished processing, remove the sorbet from the pint. Let it thaw until it is spreadable, about 5 minutes.
4. Spread the pie filling sorbet onto the frozen graham cracker crust. Spread the whipped topping on top of the filling. Freeze for 4 to 6 hours or until hardened. When ready to serve, remove from the freezer. Let the pie thaw just until you can slice it with a knife.

Green Monster Smoothie

Servings: 1 | Cooking Time: 10 Minutes

Ingredients:
- ½ cup baby spinach
- ½ apple, peeled, cored, and chopped
- ½ banana, sliced
- ¼ cup chopped carrots
- ¼ cup orange juice
- ¼ cup fresh strawberries
- ¼ cup ice

Directions:
1. Put the spinach, apples, bananas, carrots, orange juice, strawberries, and ice into an empty ninja CREAMi Pint.
2. Place the Ninja CREAMi Pint into the outer bowl. Place the outer bowl with the Pint in it into the ninja CREAMi machine and turn until the outer bowl locks into place. Push the SMOOTHIE button. During the SMOOTHIE function, the ingredients will mix together and become very creamy.
3. Once the SMOOTHIE function has ended, turn the outer bowl and release it from the ninja CREAMi machine.
4. Scoop the smoothie into a glass.

Nutrition Info:
- InfoCalories 146,Protein 2.2g,Carbohydrate 36g,Fat 0.7g,Sodium 38mg.

Oat Banana Smoothie Bowl

Servings: 2 | Cooking Time: 1 Minute

Ingredients:
- ½ cup water
- ¼ cup quick oats
- 1 cup vanilla Greek yogurt
- ½ cup banana, peeled and sliced
- 3 tablespoons honey

Directions:
1. In a small microwave-safe bowl, add the water and oats and microwave on High or about one minute.
2. Remove from the microwave and stir in the yogurt, banana and honey until well combined.
3. Transfer the mixture into an empty Ninja CREAMi pint container.
4. Cover the container with storage lid and freeze for 24 hours.
5. After 24 hours, remove the lid from container and arrange into the Outer Bowl of Ninja CREAMi.
6. Install the Creamerizer Paddle onto the lid of Outer Bowl.
7. Then rotate the lid clockwise to lock.
8. Press Power button to turn on the unit.
9. Then press Smoothie Bowl button.
10. When the program is completed, turn the Outer Bowl and release it from the machine.
11. Transfer the smoothie into serving bowls and serve with your favorite topping.

Nutrition Info:
- InfoCalories: 278,Fat: 2.7g,Carbohydrates: 55.7g,Protein: 10.9.

Piña Colada Smoothie Bowl

Servings:4 | Cooking Time:x

Ingredients:
- 1½ cups canned pineapple chunks in their juice
- ½ cup canned coconut milk
- 1 tablespoon agave nectar

Directions:
1. Pour the pineapple chunks in their juice, coconut milk, and agave into a clean CREAMi Pint and stir to combine. Place the storage lid on the container and freeze for 24 hours.
2. Remove the pint from the freezer and take off the lid. Place the pint in the outer bowl of your Ninja CREAMi, install the Creamerizer Paddle in the outer bowl lid, and lock the lid assembly onto the outer bowl. Place the bowl assembly on the motor base, and twist the handle to the right to raise the platform and lock it in place. Select the Smoothie Bowl function.
3. Once the machine has finished processing, remove the smoothie bowl from the pint. Serve immediately with your desired toppings.

Avocado & Banana Smoothie Bowl

Servings: 4 | Cooking Time:x

Ingredients:
- ½ C. unsweetened coconut milk
- ¼ C. fresh apple juice
- 2 tbsp. whey protein isolate
- 4-5 tbsp. maple syrup
- ¼ tsp. vanilla extract
- 1 C. ripe avocado, peeled, pitted and cut in ½-inch pieces
- 1 C. fresh banana, peeled and cut in ½-inch pieces

Directions:
1. In a large bowl, add the coconut milk, apple juice, protein isolate, maple syrup and vanilla extract and beat until well combined.
2. Place the avocado and banana into an empty Ninja CREAMi pint container and with the back of a spoon, firmly press the fruit below the MAX FILL line.
3. Top with coconut milk mixture and mix until well combined.
4. Cover the container with the storage lid and freeze for 24 hours.
5. After 24 hours, remove the lid from container and arrange into the outer bowl of Ninja CREAMi.
6. Install the "Creamerizer Paddle" onto the lid of outer bowl.
7. Then rotate the lid clockwise to lock.
8. Press "Power" button to turn on the unit.
9. Then press "SMOOTHIE BOWL" button.
10. When the program is completed, turn the outer bowl and release it from the machine.
11. Transfer the smoothie into serving bowls and serve immediately.

Nutrition Info:
- InfoCalories: 179,Carbohydrates: 27.2g,Protein: 1.8g,Fat: 8.7g,Sodium: 74m.

Frozen Fruit Smoothie Bowl

Servings: 2 | Cooking Time:x

Ingredients:
- 1 ripe banana, peeled and cut in 1-inch pieces
- 2 C. frozen fruit mix
- 1¼ C. vanilla yogurt

Directions:
1. In a large high-speed blender, add all the ingredients and pulse until smooth.
2. Transfer the mixture into an empty Ninja CREAMi pint container.
3. Cover the container with the storage lid and freeze for 24 hours.
4. After 24 hours, remove the lid from container and arrange into the outer bowl of Ninja CREAMi.
5. Install the "Creamerizer Paddle" onto the lid of outer bowl.
6. Then rotate the lid clockwise to lock.
7. Press "Power" button to turn on the unit.
8. Then press "SMOOTHIE BOWL" button.
9. When the program is completed, turn the outer bowl and release it from the machine.
10. Transfer the smoothie into serving bowls and serve immediately.

Nutrition Info:
- InfoCalories: 251,Carbohydrates: 45.2g,Protein: 10.8g,Fat: 2.1g,Sodium: 108m.

Avocado Smoothie

Servings: 1 | Cooking Time: 5 Minutes

Ingredients:
- ½ ripe avocado, peeled, halved, and pitted
- ½ cup milk
- ¼ cup vanilla yogurt
- 1½ tablespoons honey
- 4 ice cubes

Directions:
1. Combine the avocado, milk, yogurt, honey, and ice cubes in an empty ninja CREAMi Pint.
2. Place the Ninja CREAMi Pint into the outer bowl. Place the outer bowl with the Pint in it into the ninja CREAMi machine and turn until the outer bowl locks into place. Push the SMOOTHIE button. During the SMOOTHIE function, the ingredients will mix together and become very creamy.
3. Once the SMOOTHIE function has ended, turn the outer bowl and release it from the ninja CREAMi machine.
4. Pour the smoothie into glasses.

Nutrition Info:
- InfoCalories 96,Protein 6g,Carbohydrate 18g,Fat 0.1g,Sodium 156mg.

Fruity Coffee Smoothie Bowl

Servings: 4 | Cooking Time:x

Ingredients:
- 1 C. brewed coffee
- ½ C. oat milk
- 2 tbsp. almond butter
- 1 C. fresh raspberries
- 1 large banana, peeled and sliced

Directions:
1. In a high-speed blender add all the ingredients and pulse until smooth.
2. Transfer the mixture into an empty Ninja CREAMi pint container.
3. Cover the container with the storage lid and freeze for 24 hours.
4. After 24 hours, remove the lid from container and arrange into the outer bowl of Ninja CREAMi.
5. Install the "Creamerizer Paddle" onto the lid of outer bowl.
6. Then rotate the lid clockwise to lock.
7. Press "Power" button to turn on the unit.
8. Then press "SMOOTHIE BOWL" button.
9. When the program is completed, turn the outer bowl and release it from the machine.
10. Transfer the smoothie into serving bowls and serve immediately.

Nutrition Info:
- InfoCalories: 108,Carbohydrates: 14.9g,Protein: 3g,Fat: 5.1g,Sodium: 84m.

Pineapple & Dragon Fruit Smoothie Bowl

Servings: 2 | Cooking Time:x

Ingredients:
- 2 C. frozen dragon fruit chunks
- 2 cans pineapple juice

Directions:
1. Place the dragon fruit chunks and pineapple juice into an empty Ninja CREAMi pint container and stir to combine.
2. Cover the container with the storage lid and freeze for 24 hours.
3. After 24 hours, remove the lid from container and arrange into the outer bowl of Ninja CREAMi.
4. Install the "Creamerizer Paddle" onto the lid of outer bowl.
5. Then rotate the lid clockwise to lock.
6. Press "Power" button to turn on the unit.
7. Then press "SMOOTHIE BOWL" button.
8. When the program is completed, turn the outer bowl and release it from the machine.
9. Transfer the smoothie into serving bowls and serve immediately.

Nutrition Info:
- InfoCalories: 68,Carbohydrates: 17g,Protein: 0.3g,Fat: 0.1g,Sodium: 6m.

Strawberry-orange Creme Smoothie

Servings: 1 | Cooking Time: 5 Minutes

Ingredients:
- 1 container Yoplait Greek 100 orange creme yogurt
- ½ cup fresh strawberries, hulled
- ¼ cup ice cubes (optional)
- ¼ cup orange juice

Directions:
1. Put all the ingredients into an empty ninja CREAMi Pint.
2. Place the Ninja CREAMi Pint into the outer bowl. Place the outer bowl with the Pint in it into the ninja CREAMi machine and turn until the outer bowl locks into place. Push the SMOOTHIE button. During the SMOOTHIE function, the ingredients will mix together and become very creamy.
3. Once the SMOOTHIE function has ended, turn the outer bowl and release it from the ninja CREAMi machine.
4. Scoop the smoothie into a tall glass.

Nutrition Info:
- InfoCalories 136,Protein 12g,Carbohydrate 20g,Fat 0.3g,Sodium 103mg.

Green Fruity Smoothie Bowl

Servings: 2 | Cooking Time:x

Ingredients:
- 1 banana, peeled and cut into 1-inch pieces
- ½ of avocado, peeled, pitted and cut into 1-inch pieces
- 1 C. fresh kale leaves
- 1 C. green apple, peeled, cored and cut into 1-inch pieces
- ¼ C. unsweetened coconut milk
- 2 tbsp. agave nectar

Directions:
1. In a large high-speed blender, add all the ingredients and pulse until smooth.
2. Transfer the mixture into an empty Ninja CREAMi pint container.
3. Cover the container with the storage lid and freeze for 24 hours.
4. After 24 hours, remove the lid from container and arrange into the outer bowl of Ninja CREAMi.
5. Install the "Creamerizer Paddle" onto the lid of outer bowl.
6. Then rotate the lid clockwise to lock.
7. Press "Power" button to turn on the unit.
8. Then press "SMOOTHIE BOWL" button.
9. When the program is completed, turn the outer bowl and release it from the machine.
10. Transfer the smoothie into serving bowls and serve immediately.

Nutrition Info:
- InfoCalories: 359,Carbohydrates: 54.4g,Protein: 3.6g,Fat: 17.3g,Sodium: 24m.

Blueberry Smoothie

Servings: 1 | Cooking Time: 10 Minutes

Ingredients:
- ¾ cups Ocean Spray blueberry juice cocktail, chilled
- ⅔ cup fresh blueberries, cleaned and rinsed
- ½ cup vanilla yogurt or vanilla frozen yogurt

Directions:
1. Puree the blueberries.
2. Put the pureed blueberries, blueberry juice cocktail, and yogurt into an empty ninja CREAMi Pint
3. Place the Ninja CREAMi Pint into the outer bowl. Place the outer bowl with the Pint in it into the ninja CREAMi machine and turn until the outer bowl locks into place. Push the smoothie button. During the smoothie function, the ingredients will mix together and become very creamy.
4. Once the smoothie function has ended, turn the outer bowl and release it from the ninja CREAMi machine.
5. Scoop smoothie into a bowl.

Nutrition Info:
- InfoCalories 206,Protein 6.4g,Carbohydrate 42g,Fat 1.5g,Sodium 103mg.

Mango & Raspberry Smoothie Bowl

Servings: 2 | Cooking Time:x

Ingredients:
- ¾ cup frozen mango chunks
- ½ cup frozen raspberries
- ½ cup whole milk Greek yogurt
- 2 tablespoons avocado flesh
- 1 tablespoon agave nectar

Directions:
1. In a large bowl, add all the ingredients and mix well.
2. Transfer the mixture into an empty Ninja CREAMi pint container.
3. Cover the container with storage lid and freeze for 24 hours.
4. After 24 hours, remove the lid from container and arrange into the Outer Bowl of Ninja CREAMi.
5. Install the Creamerizer Paddle onto the lid of Outer Bowl.
6. Then rotate the lid clockwise to lock.
7. Press Power button to turn on the unit.
8. Then press Smoothie Bowl button.
9. When the program is completed, turn the Outer Bowl and release it from the machine.
10. Transfer the smoothie into serving bowls and serve immediately.

Nutrition Info:
- InfoCalories: 163,Fat: 5g,Carbohydrates: 27.4g,Protein: 3.9.

Three Fruit Smoothie Bowl

Servings: 2 | Cooking Time:x

Ingredients:
- 1 C. frozen dragon fruit pieces
- ¾ C. fresh strawberries, hulled and quartered
- ¾ C. pineapple, cut in 1-inch pieces
- ½ C. low-fat plain yogurt
- 2 tbsp. agave nectar
- 1 tbsp. fresh lime juice

Directions:
1. In a large high-speed blender, add all the ingredients and pulse until smooth.
2. Transfer the mixture into an empty Ninja CREAMi pint container.
3. Cover the container with the storage lid and freeze for 24 hours.
4. After 24 hours, remove the lid from container and arrange into the outer bowl of Ninja CREAMi.
5. Install the "Creamerizer Paddle" onto the lid of outer bowl.
6. Then rotate the lid clockwise to lock.
7. Press "Power" button to turn on the unit.
8. Then press "SMOOTHIE BOWL" button.
9. When the program is completed, turn the outer bowl and release it from the machine.
10. Transfer the smoothie into serving bowls and serve immediately.

Nutrition Info:
- InfoCalories: 183,Carbohydrates: 40.5g,Protein: 4.5g,Fat: 1.2g,Sodium: 94m.

Simple Smoothie Bowl

Servings:2 | Cooking Time:x

Ingredients:
- 1 bottle fruit smoothie beverage

Directions:
1. Pour the smoothie beverage into a clean CREAMi Pint. Place the storage lid on the container and freeze for 24 hours
2. Remove the pint from the freezer and take off the lid. Place the pint in the outer bowl of your Ninja CREAMi, install the Creamerizer Paddle in the outer bowl lid, and lock the lid assembly onto the outer bowl. Place the bowl assembly on the motor base, and twist the handle to the right to raise the platform and lock it in place. Select the Smoothie Bowl function.
3. Once the machine has finished processing, remove the smoothie bowl from the pint. Serve immediately with desired toppings.

Peaches And Cream Smoothie Bowl

Servings:4 | Cooking Time:x

Ingredients:
- 1 can peaches in their juice
- ¼ cup vanilla yogurt
- 2 tablespoons agave nectar

Directions:
1. Place the peaches in their juice, yogurt, and agave in a clean CREAMi Pint and stir to combine. Place the storage lid on the container and freeze for 24 hours.
2. Remove the pint from the freezer and take off the lid. Place the pint in the outer bowl of your Ninja CREAMi, install the Creamerizer Paddle in the outer bowl lid, and lock the lid assembly onto the outer bowl. Place the bowl assembly on the motor base, and twist the handle to the right to raise the platform and lock it in place. Select the Smoothie Bowl function.
3. Once the machine has finished processing, remove the smoothie bowl from the pint. Serve immediately with desired toppings.

Raspberry & Mango Smoothie Bowl

Servings: 2 | Cooking Time:x

Ingredients:
- ¾ C. frozen mango chunks
- ½ C. frozen raspberries
- ½ C. whole milk Greek yogurt
- 2 tbsp. avocado flesh
- 1 tbsp. agave nectar

Directions:
1. In a large bowl, add all the ingredients and mix well.
2. Transfer the mixture into an empty Ninja CREAMi pint container.
3. Cover the container with the storage lid and freeze for 24 hours.
4. After 24 hours, remove the lid from container and arrange into the outer bowl of Ninja CREAMi.
5. Install the "Creamerizer Paddle" onto the lid of outer bowl.
6. Then rotate the lid clockwise to lock.
7. Press "Power" button to turn on the unit.
8. Then press "SMOOTHIE BOWL" button.
9. When the program is completed, turn the outer bowl and release it from the machine.
10. Transfer the smoothie into serving bowls and serve immediately.

Nutrition Info:
- InfoCalories: 163,Carbohydrates: 27.4g,Protein: 3.9g,Fat: 5g,Sodium: 44m.

Raspberry Smoothie Bowl

Servings: 4 | Cooking Time:x

Ingredients:
- 1 cup brewed coffee
- ½ cup oat milk
- 2 tablespoons almond butter
- 1 cup fresh raspberries
- 1 large banana, peeled and sliced

Directions:
1. In a high-speed blender add all the ingredients and pulse until smooth.
2. Transfer the mixture into an empty Ninja CREAMi pint container.
3. Cover the container with storage lid and freeze for 24 hours.
4. After 24 hours, remove the lid from container and arrange into the Outer Bowl of Ninja CREAMi.
5. Install the Creamerizer Paddle onto the lid of Outer Bowl.
6. Then rotate the lid clockwise to lock.
7. Press Power button to turn on the unit.
8. Then press Smoothie Bowl button.
9. When the program is completed, turn the Outer Bowl and release it from the machine.
10. Transfer the smoothie into serving bowls and serve immediately.

Nutrition Info:
- InfoCalories: 108,Fat: 5.1g,Carbohydrates: 14.9g,Protein: 3.

Servings: 2 | Cooking Time:x

Ingredients:
- 1 cup frozen mango chunks
- 1 cup plain whole milk yogurt
- ¼ cup fresh orange juice
- 2 tablespoons maple syrup
- ½ teaspoon ground turmeric
- 1/8 teaspoon ground cinnamon
- 1/8 teaspoon ground ginger
- Pinch of ground black pepper

Directions:
1. In a high-speed blender, add all ingredients and pulse until smooth
2. Transfer the mixture into an empty Ninja CREAMi pint container.
3. Cover the container with storage lid and freeze for 24 hours.
4. After 24 hours, remove the lid from container and arrange into the Outer Bowl of Ninja CREAMi.
5. Install the Creamerizer Paddle onto the lid of Outer Bowl.
6. Then rotate the lid clockwise to lock.
7. Press Power button to turn on the unit.
8. Then press Smoothie Bowl button.
9. When the program is completed, turn the Outer Bowl and release it from the machine.
10. Transfer the smoothie into serving bowls and serve immediately.

Nutrition Info:
- InfoCalories: 188,Fat: 4.2g,Carbohydrates: 34.8g,Protein: 4.9.

Servings: 4 | Cooking Time:x

Ingredients:
- 1 cup cranberry juice cocktail
- ¼ cup agave nectar
- 2 cups frozen cherry berry blend

Directions:
1. In a large bowl, add the agave nectar and cranberry juice cocktail and beat until well combined.
2. Place the cherry berry blend into an empty Ninja CREAMi pint container.
3. Top with cocktail mixture and stir to combine.
4. Cover the container with storage lid and freeze for 24 hours.
5. After 24 hours, remove the lid from container and arrange into the Outer Bowl of Ninja CREAMi.
6. Install the Creamerizer Paddle onto the lid of outer bowl.
7. Then rotate the lid clockwise to lock.
8. Press Power button to turn on the unit.
9. Then press Smoothie Bowl button.
10. When the program is completed, turn the Outer Bowl and release it from the machine.
11. Transfer the smoothie into serving bowls and serve immediately.

Nutrition Info:
- InfoCalories: 127,Fat: 0.3g,Carbohydrates: 1.5g,Protein: 0.5g fresh berries, oat.

Sorbet Recipes

Sorbet Recipes

Pomegranate Sorbet Smile

Servings: 4 | Cooking Time: 24 Hours And 45 Minutes

Ingredients:
- 1 pomegranate
- ½ cup white sugar
- 1½ tablespoons freshly squeezed lemon juice
- 1½ egg whites
- 1 cup heavy whipping cream

Directions:
1. With a knife, score the pomegranate rinds lengthwise and crosswise. With the knife, carefully break open the fruit. Using the scored lines as a guide, cut the flesh into quarters with your hands. To release the seeds, hold each quarter over a big basin and beat it forcefully with a wooden spoon.
2. To release some liquid, crush the seeds in the basin with a potato masher. Continue mashing to release additional liquid after adding the sugar and lemon juice.
3. In a glass, metal, or ceramic bowl, whisk the egg whites until firm peaks form. Mash in the pomegranate mixture.
4. In a cold glass or metal bowl, beat the cream until thick. To get the correct consistency, mash it into the pomegranate mixture, popping the seeds as needed.
5. Put the mixture into the ninja CREAMi Pint container and freeze on a level surface in a cold freezer for a full 24 hours.
6. After 24 hours, remove the Pint from the freezer. Remove the lid.
7. Place the Ninja CREAMi Pint into the outer bowl. Place the outer bowl with the Pint in it into the ninja CREAMi machine and turn until the outer bowl locks into place. Push the SORBET button. During the SORBET function, the sorbet will mix together and become very creamy. This should take approximately 2 minutes.
8. Once the SORBET function has ended, turn the outer bowl and release it from the ninja CREAMi machine.
9. Your sorbet is ready to eat! Enjoy!

Nutrition Info:
- InfoCalories 386,Protein 3.6g,Carbohydrate 45g,Fat 22g,Sodium 46mg.

Chocolate Sorbet

Servings: 2 | Cooking Time: 24 Hours And 5 Minutes

Ingredients:
- ½ cup white sugar
- ⅓ cup unsweetened cocoa powder
- 1 pinch sea salt
- 1 cups water
- 1 tablespoon brewed espresso or strong coffee
- ½ teaspoon almond extract
- 1 tablespoon coffee liqueur

Directions:
1. Mix the sugar, cocoa powder, and sea salt in a large saucepan. Stir in water, espresso, and almond extract. Once the sugar has dissolved and the mixture is smooth, stir in the coffee liqueur.
2. Pour into a ninja CREAMi Pint container and freeze on a level surface in a cold freezer for a full 24 hours.
3. After 24 hours, remove the Pint from the freezer. Remove the lid.
4. Place the Ninja CREAMi Pint into the outer bowl. Place the outer bowl with the Pint in it into the ninja CREAMi machine and turn until the outer bowl locks into place. Push the SORBET button. During the SORBET function, the sorbet will mix together and become very creamy. This should take approximately 2 minutes.
5. Once the SORBET function has ended, turn the outer bowl and release it from the ninja CREAMi machine.

Nutrition Info:
- InfoCalories 256,Protein 3g,Carbohydrate 61g,Fat 2g,Sodium 63mg.

Mango Sorbet

Servings: 4 | Cooking Time:x

Ingredients:
- 4 cups mangoes, peeled, pitted and chopped
- ½ cup water
- ⅓-½ cup sugar
- ¼ cup fresh lime juice
- 2 tablespoons Chamoy

Directions:
1. In a high-speed blender, add mangoes and water and pulse until smooth.
2. Through a fine-mesh strainer, strain the mango puree into a large bowl.
3. Add the sugar, lime juice and chamoy and stir to combine.
4. Transfer the mixture into an empty Ninja CREAMi pint container.
5. Cover the container with storage lid and freeze for 24 hours.
6. After 24 hours, remove the lid from container and arrange into the Outer Bowl of Ninja CREAMi.
7. Install the Creamerizer Paddle onto the lid of Outer Bowl.
8. Then rotate the lid clockwise to lock.
9. Press Power button to turn on the unit.
10. Then press Sorbet button.
11. When the program is completed, turn the Outer Bowl and release it from the machine.
12. Transfer the sorbet into serving bowls and serve immediately.

Nutrition Info:
- InfoCalories: 168,Fat: 5.6g,Carbohydrates: 42g,Protein: 1.4.

Herbed Lemon Sorbet

Servings: 4 | Cooking Time: 6 Minutes

Ingredients:
- ½ C. water
- ¼ C. granulated sugar
- 2 large fresh dill sprigs, stemmed
- 2 large fresh basil sprigs, stemmed
- 1 C. ice water
- 2 tbsp. fresh lemon juice

Directions:
1. In a small saucepan, add sugar and water and over medium heat and cook for about 5 minutes or until the sugar is dissolved, stirring continuously.
2. Stir in the herb sprigs and remove from the heat.
3. Add the ice water and lemon juice and stir to combine.
4. Transfer the mixture into an empty Ninja CREAMi pint container.
5. Cover the container with the storage lid and freeze for 24 hours.
6. After 24 hours, remove the lid from container and arrange into the outer bowl of Ninja CREAMi.
7. Install the "Creamerizer Paddle" onto the lid of outer bowl.
8. Then rotate the lid clockwise to lock.
9. Press "Power" button to turn on the unit.
10. Then press "SORBET" button.
11. When the program is completed, turn the outer bowl and release it from the machine.
12. Transfer the sorbet into serving bowls and serve immediately.

Nutrition Info:
- InfoCalories: 51,Carbohydrates: 13.1g,Protein: 0.2g,Fat: 0.1g,Sodium: 4m.

Grape Sorbet

Servings: 4 | Cooking Time:x

Ingredients:
- ¾ cup frozen grape juice concentrate
- 1½ cups water
- 1 tablespoon fresh lemon juice

Directions:
1. In a bowl, add all the ingredients and beat until well combined.
2. Transfer the mixture into an empty Ninja CREAMi pint container.
3. Cover the container with storage lid and freeze for 24 hours.
4. After 24 hours, remove the lid from container and arrange into the Outer Bowl of Ninja CREAMi.
5. Install the Creamerizer Paddle onto the lid of Outer Bowl.
6. Then rotate the lid clockwise to lock.
7. Press Power button to turn on the unit.
8. Then press Sorbet button.
9. When the program is completed, turn the Outer Bowl and release it from the machine.
10. Transfer the sorbet into serving bowls and serve immediately.

Nutrition Info:
- InfoCalories: 25,Fat: 0.1g,Carbohydrates: 6.1g,Protein: 0.1.

Coconut Lime Sorbet

Servings: 5 | Cooking Time: 24 Hours And 30 Minutes

Ingredients:
- 1 can coconut cream
- ½ cup coconut water
- ¼ cup lime juice
- ½ tablespoon lime zest
- ¼ teaspoon coconut extract (optional)

Directions:
1. Combine the coconut cream, coconut water, lime juice, lime zest, and coconut extract in a mixing bowl. Cover with plastic wrap and refrigerate for at least 1 hour, or until the flavors have melded.
2. Add the mixture to the Ninja CREAMi Pint container and freeze on a level surface in a cold freezer for a full 24 hours.
3. After 24 hours, remove the Pint from the freezer. Remove the lid.
4. Place the Ninja CREAMi Pint into the outer bowl. Place the outer bowl with the Pint in it into the ninja CREAMi machine and turn until the outer bowl locks into place. Push the SORBET button. During the SORBET function, the sorbet will mix together and become very creamy. This should take approximately 2 minutes.
5. Once the SORBET function has ended, turn the outer bowl and release it from the ninja CREAMi machine.
6. Your sorbet is ready to eat! Enjoy!

Nutrition Info:
- InfoCalories 194,Protein 1g,Carbohydrate 30g,Fat 9g,Sodium 36mg.

Cherry-berry Rosé Sorbet

Servings: 3 | Cooking Time: 24 Hours And 10 Minutes

Ingredients:
- 2 cups frozen cherry-berry fruit blend
- ½ cup rosé wine, or as needed
- ¼ cup white sugar, or to taste
- ¼ medium lemon, juiced

Directions:
1. Add all ingredients to a bowl and mix until the sugar dissolves. Place the mixture in the ninja CREAMi Pint container and freeze on a level surface in a cold freezer for a full 24 hours.
2. After 24 hours, remove the Pint from the freezer. Remove the lid.
3. Place the Ninja CREAMi Pint into the outer bowl. Place the outer bowl with the Pint in it into the ninja CREAMi machine and turn until the outer bowl locks into place. Push the SORBET button. During the SORBET function, the sorbet will mix together and become very creamy. This should take approximately 2 minutes.
4. Once the SORBET function has ended, turn the outer bowl and release it from the ninja CREAMi machine.
5. Your sorbet is ready to eat! Enjoy!

Nutrition Info:
- InfoCalories 186,Protein 1.5g,Carbohydrate 40g,Fat 0.2g,Sodium 4.9mg.

Strawberries & Champagne Sorbet

Servings: 3 | Cooking Time: 24 Hours And 15 Minutes

Ingredients:
- 1 packet strawberry-flavored gelatin (such as Jell-O)
- ¾ cup boiling water
- ½ cup light corn syrup
- 3 fluid ounces champagne
- 1 egg whites, slightly beaten

Directions:
1. Dissolve the gelatin in boiling water in a bowl. Beat in the corn syrup, champagne, and egg whites.
2. Put the mixture into the ninja CREAMi Pint container and freeze on a level surface in a cold freezer for a full 24 hours.
3. After 24 hours, remove the Pint from the freezer. Remove the lid.
4. Place the Ninja CREAMi Pint into the outer bowl. Place the outer bowl with the Pint in it into the ninja CREAMi machine and turn until the outer bowl locks into place. Push the SORBET button. During the SORBET function, the sorbet will mix together and become very creamy. This should take approximately 2 minutes.
5. Once the SORBET function has ended, turn the outer bowl and release it from the ninja CREAMi machine.
6. Your sorbet is ready to eat! Enjoy!

Nutrition Info:
- InfoCalories 196,Protein 2.5g,Carbohydrate 46g,Fat 5g,Sodium 106mg.

Pineapple Sorbet

Servings: 1 | Cooking Time: 24 Hours 5 Minutes

Ingredients:
- 12 ounces canned pineapple

Directions:
1. Pour the pineapple, with the liquid from the can, into a ninja CREAMi Pint container and freeze on a level surface in a cold freezer for a full 24 hours.
2. After 24 hours, remove the Pint from the freezer. Remove the lid.
3. Place the Ninja CREAMi Pint into the outer bowl. Place the outer bowl with the Pint in it into the ninja CREAMi machine and turn until the outer bowl locks into place. Push the SORBET button. During the SORBET function, the sorbet will mix together and become very creamy. This should take approximately 2 minutes.
4. Once the SORBET function has ended, turn the outer bowl and release it from the ninja CREAMi machine.
5. Your sorbet is ready to eat! Enjoy!

Nutrition Info:
- InfoCalories 276,Protein 2g,Carbohydrate 71g,Fat 1g,Sodium 56mg.

Celery Sorbet

Servings: 3 | Cooking Time: 24 Hours And 5 Minutes

Ingredients:
- ½ cup white sugar
- ½ cup cold water
- ½ pound trimmed celery
- Pinch of salt, or to taste
- ½ medium lime, juiced

Directions:
1. In a saucepan over medium heat, combine the sugar and water until it just begins to boil. Remove the pan from the heat. While the other ingredients are being prepared, cool the simple syrup to room temperature.
2. The celery should be cut into tiny pieces. Combine the salt, lime juice, and the cooled simple syrup in a mixing bowl. Blend until completely smooth.
3. Fill a sieve with the mixture. Using a spoon, press the mixture through the strainer until all of the juice has been removed. Cover and refrigerate the juice for at least 1 hour or until completely cooled.
4. Put the cooled mixture into the ninja CREAMi Pint container and freeze on a level surface in a cold freezer for a full 24 hours.
5. After 24 hours, remove the Pint from the freezer. Remove the lid.
6. Place the Ninja CREAMi Pint into the outer bowl. Place the outer bowl with the Pint in it into the ninja CREAMi machine and turn until the outer bowl locks into place. Push the SORBET button. During the SORBET function, the sorbet will mix together and become very creamy. This should take approximately 2 minutes.
7. Once the SORBET function has ended, turn the outer bowl and release it from the ninja CREAMi machine.
8. Your sorbet is ready to eat! Enjoy!

Nutrition Info:
- InfoCalories 146,Protein 0.6g,Carbohydrate 38g,Fat 0.2g,Sodium 116mg.

Lime Sorbet

Servings: 4 | Cooking Time:x

Ingredients:
- ¾ cup beer
- ⅔ cup water
- ½ cup fresh lime juice
- ¼ cup granulated sugar

Directions:
1. In a high-speed blender, add all the ingredients and pulse until smooth.
2. Set aside for about five minutes.
3. Transfer the mixture into an empty Ninja CREAMi pint container.
4. Cover the container with storage lid and freeze for 24 hours.
5. After 24 hours, remove the lid from container and arrange into the Outer Bowl of Ninja CREAMi.
6. Install the Creamerizer Paddle onto the lid of Outer Bowl.
7. Then rotate the lid clockwise to lock.
8. Press Power button to turn on the unit.
9. Then press Sorbet button.
10. When the program is completed, turn the Outer Bowl and release it from the machine.
11. Transfer the sorbet into serving bowls and serve immediately.

Nutrition Info:
- InfoCalories: 69,Fat: 0g,Carbohydrates: 14.4g,Protein: 0.2.

Mojito Sorbet

Servings: 8 | Cooking Time: 24 Hours And 5 Minutes

Ingredients:
- ½ cup water
- ½ cup white sugar
- ¼ cup mint leaves, packed
- 1 teaspoon grated lime zest
- ½ cup freshly squeezed lime juice
- ¾ cup citrus-flavored sparkling water
- 1 tablespoon rum (optional)

Directions:
1. Add all ingredients to a bowl and mix until the sugar is dissolved. Pour into the ninja CREAMi Pint container and freeze on a level surface in a cold freezer for a full 24 hours.
2. After 24 hours, remove the Pint from the freezer. Remove the lid.
3. Place the Ninja CREAMi Pint into the outer bowl. Place the outer bowl with the Pint in it into the ninja CREAMi machine and turn until the outer bowl locks into place. Push the SORBET button. During the SORBET function, the sorbet will mix together and become very creamy. This should take approximately 2 minutes.
4. Once the SORBET function has ended, turn the outer bowl and release it from the ninja CREAMi machine.
5. Your sorbet is ready to eat! Enjoy!

Nutrition Info:
- InfoCalories 56,Protein 0.1g,Carbohydrate 14g,Fat 0.1g,Sodium 1.6mg.

Banana Sorbet

Servings: 2 | Cooking Time: 24 Hours And 5 Minutes

Ingredients:
- 1 frozen banana
- 1 teaspoon cold water
- 2 teaspoons caramel sauce

Directions:
1. Add the banana, water, and caramel sauce into the ninja CREAMi Pint container and freeze on a level surface in a cold freezer for a full 24 hours.
2. After 24 hours, remove the Pint from the freezer. Remove the lid.
3. Place the Ninja CREAMi Pint into the outer bowl. Place the outer bowl with the Pint in it into the ninja CREAMi machine and turn until the outer bowl locks into place. Push the SORBET button. During the SORBET function, the sorbet will mix together and become very creamy. This should take approximately 2 minutes.
4. Once the SORBET function has ended, turn the outer bowl and release it from the ninja CREAMi machine.

Nutrition Info:
- InfoCalories 70,Protein 0.7g,Carbohydrate 18g,Fat 0.2g,Sodium 25mg.

Cherry Sorbet

Servings: 4 | Cooking Time:x

Ingredients:
- 1½ C. cola
- 1/3 C. maraschino cherries
- 1/3 C. spiced rum
- ¼ C. water
- 1 tbsp. fresh lime juice

Directions:
1. In a high-speed blender, add all the ingredients and pulse until smooth.
2. Transfer the mixture into an empty Ninja CREAMi pint container.
3. Cover the container with the storage lid and freeze for 24 hours.
4. After 24 hours, remove the lid from container and arrange into the outer bowl of Ninja CREAMi.
5. Install the "Creamerizer Paddle" onto the lid of outer bowl.
6. Then rotate the lid clockwise to lock.
7. Press "Power" button to turn on the unit.
8. Then press "SORBET" button.
9. When the program is completed, turn the outer bowl and release it from the machine.
10. Transfer the sorbet into serving bowls and serve immediately.

Nutrition Info:
- InfoCalories: 95,Carbohydrates: 13.4g,Protein: 0.2g,Fat: 0.1g,Sodium: 4m.

Lemony Herb Sorbet

Servings: 4 | Cooking Time: 6 Minutes

Ingredients:
- ½ cup water
- ¼ cup granulated sugar
- 2 large fresh dill sprigs, stemmed
- 2 large fresh basil sprigs, stemmed
- 1 cup ice water
- 2 tablespoons fresh lemon juice

Directions:
1. In a small saucepan, add sugar and water and over medium heat and cook for about five minutes or until the sugar is dissolved, stirring continuously.
2. Stir in the herb sprigs and remove from the heat.
3. Add the ice water and lemon juice and stir to combine.
4. Transfer the mixture into an empty Ninja CREAMi pint container.
5. Cover the container with storage lid and freeze for 24 hours.
6. After 24 hours, remove the lid from container and arrange into the Outer Bowl of Ninja CREAMi.
7. Install the Creamerizer Paddle onto the lid of Outer Bowl.
8. Then rotate the lid clockwise to lock.
9. Press Power button to turn on the unit.
10. Then press Sorbet button.
11. When the program is completed, turn the Outer Bowl and release it from the machine.
12. Transfer the sorbet into serving bowls and serve immediately.

Nutrition Info:
- InfoCalories: 51,Fat: 0.1g,Carbohydrates: 13.1g,Protein: 0.2.

Acai & Fruit Sorbet

Servings: 4 | Cooking Time:x

Ingredients:
- 1 packet frozen acai
- ½ cup blackberries
- ½ cup banana, peeled and sliced
- ¼ cup granulated sugar
- 1 cup water

Directions:
1. In a high-speed blender, add all the ingredients and pulse until smooth.
2. Transfer the mixture into an empty Ninja CREAMi pint container.
3. Cover the container with storage lid and freeze for 24 hours.
4. After 24 hours, remove the lid from container and arrange into the Outer Bowl of Ninja CREAMi.
5. Install the Creamerizer Paddle onto the lid of Outer Bowl.
6. Then rotate the lid clockwise to lock.
7. Press Power button to turn on the unit.
8. Then press Sorbet button.
9. When the program is completed, turn the Outer Bowl and release it from the machine.
10. Transfer the sorbet into serving bowls and serve immediately.

Nutrition Info:
- InfoCalories: 86,Fat: 0.2g,Carbohydrates: 22.3g,Protein: 0.5.

Blueberry Lemon Sorbet

Servings: 1 | Cooking Time: 24 Hours And 5 Minutes

Ingredients:
- 1 tablespoon cream cheese
- ¼ cup milk
- 1½ cups lemonade
- ⅓ cup blueberries (fresh or frozen)

Directions:
1. In a medium mixing bowl, whisk together the softened cream cheese and the milk. Make an effort to integrate the two as much as possible. Some little bits of cream cheese may remain, but that's fine as long as they're small.
2. Add the lemonade and stir thoroughly.
3. Pour the mixture into a ninja CREAMi Pint container, add the blueberries and freeze on a level surface in a cold freezer for a full 24 hours.
4. After 24 hours, remove the Pint from the freezer. Remove the lid.
5. Place the Ninja CREAMi Pint into the outer bowl. Place the outer bowl with the Pint in it into the ninja CREAMi machine and turn until the outer bowl locks into place. Push the SORBET button. During the SORBET function, the sorbet will mix together and become very creamy. This should take approximately 2 minutes.
6. Once the SORBET function has ended, turn the outer bowl and release it from the ninja CREAMi machine.
7. Your sorbet is ready to eat! Enjoy!
8. Place the outer bowl with the Pint back into the ninja CREAMi machine and lock it into place if the sorbet isn't quite creamy enough. Select the RE-SPIN option. Remove the outer bowl from the Ninja CREAMi after the RE-SPIN cycle is complete.

Nutrition Info:
- InfoCalories 246,Protein 3g,Carbohydrate 56g,Fat 7g,Sodium 96mg.

Pineapple Rum Sorbet

Servings: 4 | Cooking Time:x

Ingredients:
- ¾ C. piña colada mix
- ¼ C. rum
- 2 tbsp. granulated sugar
- 1½ C. frozen pineapple chunks

Directions:
1. In a high-speed blender, add all the ingredients and pulse until smooth.
2. Transfer the mixture into an empty Ninja CREAMi pint container.
3. Cover the container with the storage lid and freeze for 24 hours.
4. After 24 hours, remove the lid from container and arrange into the outer bowl of Ninja CREAMi.
5. Install the "Creamerizer Paddle" onto the lid of outer bowl.
6. Then rotate the lid clockwise to lock.
7. Press "Power" button to turn on the unit.
8. Then press "SORBET" button.
9. When the program is completed, turn the outer bowl and release it from the machine.
10. Transfer the sorbet into serving bowls and serve immediately.

Nutrition Info:
- InfoCalories: 102,Carbohydrates: 17.6g,Protein: 0.6g,Fat: 0.2g,Sodium: 1m.

Avocado Lime Sorbet

Servings: 4 | Cooking Time: 5 Minutes

Ingredients:
- ¾ C. water
- 2 tbsp. light corn syrup
- Pinch of sea salt
- 2/3 C. granulated sugar
- 1 large ripe avocado, peeled, pitted and chopped
- 3 oz. fresh lime juice

Directions:
1. In a medium saucepan, add water, corn syrup and salt and beat until well combined.
2. Place the saucepan over medium heat.
3. Slowly add the sugar, continuously beating until well combined and bring to a boil.
4. Remove the saucepan from heat and set aside to cool completely.
5. In a high-speed blender, add the sugar mixture, avocado and lime juice and pulse until smooth.
6. Transfer the mixture into an empty Ninja CREAMi pint container.
7. Cover the container with the storage lid and freeze for 24 hours.
8. After 24 hours, remove the lid from container and arrange into the outer bowl of Ninja CREAMi.
9. Install the "Creamerizer Paddle" onto the lid of outer bowl.
10. Then rotate the lid clockwise to lock.
11. Press "Power" button to turn on the unit.
12. Then press "SORBET" button.
13. When the program is completed, turn the outer bowl and release it from the machine.
14. Transfer the sorbet into serving bowls and serve immediately.

Nutrition Info:
- InfoCalories: 244,Carbohydrates: 46g,Protein: 0.9g,Fat: 8.3g,Sodium: 64m.

Mixed Berries Sorbet

Servings: 4 | Cooking Time:x

Ingredients:
- 1 cup blueberries
- 1 cup raspberries
- 1 cup strawberries, hulled and quartered

Directions:
1. In an empty Ninja CREAMi pint container, place the berries and with a potato masher, mash until well combined.
2. Cover the container with storage lid and freeze for 24 hours.
3. After 24 hours, remove the lid from container and arrange into the outer bowl of Ninja CREAMi.
4. Install the Creamerizer Paddle onto the lid of Outer Bowl.
5. Then rotate the lid clockwise to lock.
6. Press Power button to turn on the unit.
7. Then press Sorbet button.
8. When the program is completed, turn the Outer Bowl and release it from the machine.
9. Transfer the sorbet into serving bowls and serve immediately.

Nutrition Info:
- InfoCalories: 48,Fat: .40g,Carbohydrates: 11.7g,Protein: 0.9.

Italian Ice Sorbet

Servings: 1 | Cooking Time: 24 Hours And 5 Minutes

Ingredients:
- 12 ounces lemonade
- Sugar or your preferred sweetener to taste (optional)
- If the lemonade you're using is quite tart, use 6 ounces of lemonade and 6 ounces of water instead of 12 ounces of lemonade

Directions:
1. Pour the lemonade (or lemonade and water mixture) into a ninja CREAMi Pint container and freeze on a level surface in a cold freezer for a full 24 hours.
2. After 24 hours, remove the Pint from the freezer. Remove the lid.
3. Place the Ninja CREAMi Pint into the outer bowl. Place the outer bowl with the Pint in it into the ninja CREAMi machine and turn until the outer bowl locks into place. Push the SORBET button. During the SORBET function, the sorbet will mix together and become very creamy. This should take approximately 2 minutes.
4. Once the SORBET function has ended, turn the outer bowl and release it from the ninja CREAMi machine.

Nutrition Info:
- InfoCalories 236,Protein 8g,Carbohydrate 58g,Fat 14g,Sodium 29mg.

Raspberry Lime Sorbet

Servings: 4 | Cooking Time:x

Ingredients:
- 2 C. fresh raspberries
- 5 oz. simple syrup
- 6 tbsp. fresh lime juice

Directions:
1. In an empty Ninja CREAMi pint container, add all the ingredients and mix well.
2. Cover the container with the storage lid and freeze for 24 hours.
3. After 24 hours, remove the lid from container and arrange into the outer bowl of Ninja CREAMi.
4. Install the "Creamerizer Paddle" onto the lid of outer bowl.
5. Then rotate the lid clockwise to lock.
6. Press "Power" button to turn on the unit.
7. Then press "SORBET" button.
8. When the program is completed, turn the outer bowl and release it from the machine.
9. Transfer the sorbet into serving bowls and serve immediately.

Nutrition Info:
- InfoCalories: 147,Carbohydrates: 37.3g,Protein: 0.7g,Fat: 0.4g,Sodium: 26m.

Pear Sorbet

Servings: 4 | Cooking Time:x

Ingredients:
- 1 can pears in light syrup

Directions:
1. Place the pear pieces into an empty Ninja CREAMi to the MAX FILL line.
2. Cover the orange pieces with syrup from the can.
3. Cover the container with the storage lid and freeze for 24 hours.
4. After 24 hours, remove the lid from container and arrange into the outer bowl of Ninja CREAMi.
5. Install the "Creamerizer Paddle" onto the lid of outer bowl.
6. Then rotate the lid clockwise to lock.
7. Press "Power" button to turn on the unit.
8. Then press "SORBET" button.
9. When the program is completed, turn the outer bowl and release it from the machine.
10. Transfer the sorbet into serving bowls and serve immediately.

Nutrition Info:
- InfoCalories: 63,Carbohydrates: 16.5g,Protein: 0.4g,Fat: 0.2g,Sodium: 2m.

Ice Cream Recipes

Ice Cream Recipes

Coffee Ice Cream

Servings: 4 | Cooking Time:x

Ingredients:
- ¾ cup coconut cream
- ½ cup granulated sugar
- 1½ tablespoons instant coffee powder
- 1 cup rice milk
- 1 teaspoon vanilla extract

Directions:
1. In a bowl, add coconut cream and beat until smooth.
2. Add the remaining ingredients and beat sugar is dissolved.
3. Transfer the mixture into an empty Ninja CREAMi pint container.
4. Cover the container with storage lid and freeze for 24 hours.
5. After 24 hours, remove the lid from container and arrange into the Outer Bowl of Ninja CREAMi.
6. Install the Creamerizer Paddle onto the lid of Outer Bowl.
7. Then rotate the lid clockwise to lock.
8. Press Power button to turn on the unit.
9. Then press Ice Cream button.
10. When the program is completed, turn the Outer Bowl and release it from the machine.
11. Transfer the ice cream into serving bowls and serve immediately.

Nutrition Info:
- InfoCalories: 230,Fat: 11.2g,Carbohydrates: 33.8g,Protein: 1.1.

Mango Ice Cream

Servings: 1 | Cooking Time: 24 Hours And 5 Minutes

Ingredients:
- 1 mango (medium-sized, cut into quarters)
- 1 tablespoon cream cheese (room temperature)
- ¼ cup sugar
- ¾ cup heavy whipping cream
- 1 cup milk

Directions:
1. Combine the cream cheese, sugar in a mixing bowl. Using a whisk, mix together until all ingredients are thoroughly combined, and the sugar starts to dissolve.
2. Add in the heavy whipping cream and milk. Whisk until all ingredients have combined well.
3. Pour mixture into an empty ninja CREAMi Pint container. Freeze for 24 hours after adding the mango to the Pint, ensuring you don't go over the maximum fill line.
4. Take the Pint out of the freezer after 24 hours. Take off the cover.
5. Place the Ninja CREAMi Pint into the outer bowl. Place the outer bowl with the Pint in it into the ninja CREAMi machine and turn until the outer bowl locks into place. Push the ICE CREAM button. During the ICE CREAM function, the ice cream will mix and become very creamy.
6. Once the ICE CREAM function has ended, turn the outer bowl and release it from the ninja CREAMi machine.

Nutrition Info:
- InfoCalories 96,Protein 6g,Carbohydrate 18g,Fat 0.1g,Sodium 156mg.

Fruity Extract Ice Cream

Servings: 4 | Cooking Time:x

Ingredients:
- 1 cup whole milk
- ¾ cup heavy cream
- 2 tablespoons monk fruit sweetener with Erythritol
- 2 tablespoons agave nectar
- ½ teaspoon raspberry extract
- ½ teaspoon vanilla extract
- ¼ teaspoon lemon extract
- 5-6 drops blue food coloring

Directions:
1. In a bowl, add all ingredients and eat until well combined.
2. Transfer the mixture into an empty Ninja CREAMi pint container.
3. Cover the container with storage lid and freeze for 24 hours.
4. After 24 hours, remove the lid from container and arrange into the Outer Bowl of Ninja CREAMi.
5. Install the Creamerizer Paddle onto the lid of outer bowl.
6. Then rotate the lid clockwise to lock.
7. Press Power button to turn on the unit.
8. Then press Ice Cream button.
9. When the program is completed, turn the Outer Bowl and release it from the machine.
10. Transfer the ice cream into serving bowls and serve immediately.

Nutrition Info:
- InfoCalories: 147,Fat: 10.3g,Carbohydrates: 11.6g,Protein: 2.4.

Super Lemon Ice Cream

Servings: 5 | Cooking Time: 24 Hours And 20 Minutes

Ingredients:
- 1 cup heavy whipping cream
- ½ cup half-and-half cream
- ½ cup white sugar
- 1 tablespoon grated lemon zest
- 2 egg yolks
- ¼ cup fresh lemon juice

Directions:
1. On low heat, whisk together the heavy cream, half-and-half cream, sugar, and lemon zest in a saucepan until the sugar is dissolved.
2. In a mixing dish, whisk together the egg yolks.
3. Stir in a few tablespoons of the cream mixture at a time into the eggs. This will assist in bringing the eggs up to temperature without them becoming scrambled. Return the egg mixture to the bowl with the cream mixture.
4. Pour the mixture into an empty ninja CREAMi Pint container, add lemon, and freeze for 24 hours.
5. After 24 hours, remove the Pint from the freezer. Remove the lid.
6. Place the Ninja CREAMi Pint into the outer bowl. Place the outer bowl with the Pint in it into the ninja CREAMi machine and turn until the outer bowl locks into place. Push the ICE CREAM button.
7. Once the ICE CREAM function has ended, turn the outer bowl and release it from the ninja CREAMi machine.

Nutrition Info:
- InfoCalories 316,Protein 3.7g,Carbohydrate 27g,Fat 22g,Sodium 36mg.

Peanut Butter Ice Cream

Servings: 4 | Cooking Time:x

Ingredients:
- 1¾ cups skim milk
- 3 tablespoons smooth peanut butter
- ¼ cup stevia-cane sugar blend
- 1 teaspoon vanilla extract

Directions:
1. In a bowl, add all ingredients and beat until smooth.
2. Set aside for about five minutes.
3. Transfer the mixture into an empty Ninja CREAMi pint container.
4. Cover the container with storage lid and freeze for 24 hours.
5. After 24 hours, remove the lid from container and arrange into the outer bowl of Ninja CREAMi.
6. Install the Creamerizer Paddle onto the lid of Outer Bowl.
7. Then rotate the lid clockwise to lock.
8. Press Power button to turn on the unit.
9. Then press Ice Cream button.
10. When the program is completed, turn the Outer Bowl and release it from the machine.
11. Transfer the ice cream into serving bowls and serve immediately.

Nutrition Info:
- InfoCalories: 143,Fat: 6.1g,Carbohydrates: 19.7g,Protein: 6.5.

'pea'nut Butter Ice Cream

Servings:4 | Cooking Time:x

Ingredients:
- ½ cup frozen peas, thawed
- ½ cup plus 1 tablespoon granulated sugar
- 1 tablespoon corn syrup
- 2 tablespoons powdered peanut butter
- 1 cup whole milk
- 1 teaspoon vanilla extract
- ⅓ cup heavy (whipping) cream

Directions:
1. Combine the peas, sugar, corn syrup, powdered peanut butter, milk, and vanilla in a blender. Blend on high until smooth.
2. Pour the base into a clean CREAMi Pint. Whisk in the heavy cream until combined. Place the storage lid on the container and freeze for 24 hours.
3. Remove the CREAMi Pint from the freezer and take off the lid. Place the pint in outer bowl of your Ninja CREAMi, install the Creamerizer Paddle in the outer bowl lid, and lock the lid assembly onto the outer bowl. Place the bowl assembly on the motor base, and twist the handle to the right to raise the platform and lock it in place. Select the Ice Cream function.
4. Once the machine has finished processing, remove the ice cream from the pint. Serve immediately.

Coconut Ice Cream

Servings: 4 | Cooking Time: 24 Hours And 5 Minutes

Ingredients:
- ½ cup milk
- 1 can cream of coconut
- ¾ cup heavy cream
- ½ cup sweetened flaked coconut

Directions:
1. In a food processor or blender, combine the milk and coconut cream and thoroughly mix.
2. Combine the heavy cream and flaked coconut in a mixing bowl, and then add to the milk-cream mixture. Combine well.
3. Pour the mixture into an empty ninja CREAMi Pint container and freeze for 24 hours.
4. After 24 hours, remove the Pint from the freezer. Remove the lid.
5. Place the Ninja CREAMi Pint into the outer bowl. Place the outer bowl with the Pint in it into the ninja CREAMi machine and turn until the outer bowl locks into place. Push the ICE CREAM button.
6. Once the ICE CREAM function has ended, turn the outer bowl and release it from the ninja CREAMi machine.

Nutrition Info:
- InfoCalories 406,Protein 3g,Carbohydrate 36g,Fat 29g,Sodium 86mg.

Lemon Ice Cream

Servings: 4 | Cooking Time:x

Ingredients:
- 1 can full-fat unsweetened coconut milk
- ½ cup granulated sugar
- 1 teaspoon vanilla extract
- 1 teaspoon lemon extract

Directions:
1. In a bowl, add the coconut milk and beat until smooth.
2. Add the remaining ingredients and beat until sugar is dissolved.
3. Transfer the mixture into an empty Ninja CREAMi pint container.
4. Cover the container with storage lid and freeze for 24 hours.
5. After 24 hours, remove the lid from container and arrange into the Outer Bowl of Ninja CREAMi.
6. Install the Creamerizer Paddle onto the lid of Outer Bowl.
7. Then rotate the lid clockwise to lock.
8. Press Power button to turn on the unit.
9. Then press Ice Cream button.
10. When the program is completed, turn the Outer Bowl and release it from the machine.
11. Transfer the ice cream into serving bowls and serve immediately.

Nutrition Info:
- InfoCalories: 280,Fat: 18.3g,Carbohydrates: 28.2g,Protein: 1.5.

Strawberry Ice Cream

Servings: 4 | Cooking Time:x

Ingredients:
- ¼ cup sugar
- 1 tablespoon cream cheese, softened
- 1 teaspoon vanilla bean paste
- 1 cup milk
- ¾ cup heavy whipping cream
- 6 medium fresh strawberries, hulled and quartered

Directions:
1. In a bowl, add the sugar, cream cheese, vanilla bean paste and with a wire whisk, mix until well combined.
2. Add in the milk and heavy whipping cream and beat until well combined.
3. Transfer the mixture into an empty Ninja CREAMi pint container.
4. Add the strawberry pieces and stir to combine.
5. Cover the container with storage lid and freeze for 24 hours.
6. After 24 hours, remove the lid from container and arrange into the Outer Bowl of Ninja CREAMi.
7. Install the Creamerizer Paddle onto the lid of Outer Bowl.
8. Then rotate the lid clockwise to lock.
9. Press Power button to turn on the unit.
10. Then press Ice Cream button.
11. When the program is completed, turn the Outer Bowl and release it from the machine.
12. Transfer the ice cream into serving bowls and serve immediately.

Nutrition Info:
- InfoCalories: 175,Fat: 10.5g,Carbohydrates: 18.8g,Protein: 2.8.

French Vanilla Ice Cream

Servings:4 | Cooking Time:x

Ingredients:
- 4 large egg yolks
- 1 tablespoon light corn syrup
- ¼ cup plus 1 tablespoon granulated sugar
- ⅓ cup whole milk
- 1 cup heavy (whipping) cream
- 1 teaspoon vanilla extract

Directions:
1. Fill a large bowl with ice water and set it aside.
2. In a small saucepan, whisk together the egg yolks, corn syrup, and sugar until the mixture is fully combined and the sugar is dissolved. Do not do this over heat.
3. Whisk in the milk, heavy cream, and vanilla until combined.
4. Place the pan over medium heat. Cook, stirring constantly with a rubber spatula, until the temperature reaches 165°F to 175°F on an instant-read thermometer.
5. Remove the pan from the heat and pour the base through a fine-mesh strainer into a clean CREAMi Pint. Carefully place the container in the prepared ice water bath, making sure the water doesn't spill into the base.
6. Once the base has cooled, place the storage lid on the pint and freeze for 24 hours.
7. Remove the CREAMi Pint from the freezer and take off the lid. Place the pint in the outer bowl of your Ninja CREAMi, install the Creamerizer Paddle in the outer bowl lid, and lock the lid assembly onto the outer bowl. Place the bowl assembly on the motor base, and twist the handle to the right to raise the platform and lock it in place. Select the Ice Cream function.
8. Once the machine has finished processing, remove the ice cream from the pint. Serve immediately.

Classic Vanilla Ice Cream

Servings:4 | Cooking Time:x

Ingredients:
- 1 tablespoon cream cheese, at room temperature
- ⅓ cup granulated sugar
- 1 teaspoon vanilla extract
- ¾ cup heavy (whipping) cream
- 1 cup whole milk
- ¼ cup mini chocolate chips (optional)

Directions:
1. In a large microwave-safe bowl, add the cream cheese and microwave for 10 seconds. Add the sugar and vanilla extract, and with a whisk or rubber spatula, combine the mixture until it looks like frosting, about 60 seconds.
2. Slowly whisk in the heavy cream and milk and mix until the sugar is completely dissolved and the cream cheese is completely incorporated.
3. Pour the base into a clean CREAMi Pint. Place the storage lid on the container and freeze for 24 hours.
4. Remove the CREAMi Pint from the freezer and take off the lid. Place the pint container in the outer bowl of your Ninja CREAMi, install the Creamerizer Paddle in the outer bowl lid, and lock the lid assembly onto the outer bowl. Place the bowl assembly on the motor base, and twist the handle to the right to raise the platform and lock it in place. Select the Ice Cream function.
5. Once the machine has finished processing, remove the lid from the pint container. If you are adding chocolate chips: with a spoon, create a 1½-inch-wide hole that reaches the bottom of the pint. During this process, it is okay if your treat reaches above the Max Fill line. Add ¼ cup of mini chocolate chips to the hole in the pint, replace the lid, and select the Mix-In function.
6. Serve immediately with desired toppings.

Chocolate Ice Cream

Servings: 1 | Cooking Time: 24 Hours And 5 Minutes

Ingredients:
- ¾ cup heavy whipping cream
- ½ can sweetened condensed milk
- ½ cup unsweetened cocoa powder
- ½ teaspoon vanilla extract

Directions:
1. In a medium mixing bowl, combine the sweetened condensed milk, cocoa powder, and vanilla extract.
2. In a separate bowl, whip the heavy cream until it forms firm peaks (do not overbeat).
3. Pour mixture into an empty ninja CREAMi Pint container and freeze for 24 hours.
4. After 24 hours, remove the Pint from the freezer. Remove the lid.
5. Place the Ninja CREAMi Pint into the outer bowl. Place the outer bowl with the Pint in it into the ninja CREAMi machine and turn until the outer bowl locks into place. Push the ICE CREAM button. During the ICE CREAM function, the ice cream will mix together and become very creamy.
6. Once the ICE CREAM function has ended, turn the outer bowl and release it from the ninja CREAMi machine.

Nutrition Info:
- InfoCalories 96,Protein 6g,Carbohydrate 18g,Fat 0.1g,Sodium 156mg.

Pear Ice Cream

Servings: 4 | Cooking Time: 15 Minutes

Ingredients:
- 3 medium ripe pears, peeled, cored and cut into 1-inch pieces
- 1 can full-fat unsweetened coconut milk
- ½ cup granulated sugar

Directions:
1. In a medium saucepan, add all ingredients and stir to combine.
2. Place the saucepan over medium heat and bring to a boil.
3. Reduce the heat to low and simmer for about ten minutes or until liquid is reduced by half.
4. Remove from the heat and set aside to cool.
5. After cooling, transfer the mixture into a high-speed blender and pulse until smooth.
6. Transfer the mixture into an empty Ninja CREAMi pint container.
7. Cover the container with storage lid and freeze for 24 hours.
8. After 24 hours, remove the lid from container and arrange into the Outer Bowl of Ninja CREAMi.
9. Install the Creamerizer Paddle onto the lid of Outer Bowl.
10. Then rotate the lid clockwise to lock.
11. Press Power button to turn on the unit.
12. Then press Ice Cream button.
13. When the program is completed, turn the Outer Bowl and release it from the machine.
14. Transfer the ice cream into serving bowls and serve immediately.

Nutrition Info:
- InfoCalories: 368,Fat: 18.5g,Carbohydrates: 51.9g,Protein: 2.1.

Coconut-vanilla Ice Cream

Servings:4 | Cooking Time:x

Ingredients:
- 1 can full-fat unsweetened coconut milk
- ½ cup organic sugar
- 1 teaspoon vanilla extract

Directions:
1. In a large bowl, whisk together the coconut milk, sugar, and vanilla until everything is incorporated and the sugar is dissolved.
2. Pour the base into a clean CREAMi Pint. Place the storage lid on the container and freeze for 24 hours.
3. Remove the CREAMi Pint from the freezer and take off the lid. Place the pint in the outer bowl of your Ninja CREAMi, install the Creamerizer Paddle in the outer bowl lid, and lock the lid assembly onto the outer bowl. Place the bowl assembly on the motor base, and twist the handle to the right to raise the platform and lock it in place. Select the Ice Cream function.
4. Once the machine has finished processing, remove the ice cream from the pint. Serve immediately with desired toppings.

Cinnamon Red Hot Ice Cream

Servings: 5 | Cooking Time: 24 Hours And 10 Minutes

Ingredients:
- 2 cups heavy whipping cream, divided
- 1 egg yolk
- 1 cup half-and-half
- ½ cup Red Hot candies

Directions:
1. In a mixing bowl, whisk together 1 cup of cream and the egg yolks until smooth.
2. In another large bowl, combine the half-and-half, 1 cup cream, and Red Hot candies. Whisk with a wooden spoon until the candies dissolve, about 5 to 10 minutes.
3. Pour the cream-egg mixture into the candy mixture and stir to incorporate.
4. Pour the mixture into an empty ninja CREAMi Pint container and freeze for 24 hours.
5. After 24 hours, remove the Pint from the freezer. Remove the lid.
6. Place the Ninja CREAMi Pint into the outer bowl. Place the outer bowl with the Pint in it into the ninja CREAMi machine and turn until the outer bowl locks into place. Push the ICE CREAM button.
7. Once the ICE CREAM function has ended, turn the outer bowl and release it from the ninja CREAMi machine.

Nutrition Info:
- InfoCalories 322,Protein 3g,Carbohydrate 24.5g,Fat 24g,Sodium 106mg.

Raspberry White Truffle Ice Cream

Servings: 1 | Cooking Time: 24 Hours And 5 Minutes

Ingredients:
- Ice cream base:
- 1 tablespoon cream cheese (room temperature)
- ⅓ cup sugar
- 1 tablespoon raspberry preserves
- ¾ cup heavy whipping cream
- 1 cup milk
- ¼ cup raspberries (cut in half)
- Mix-ins:(optional)
- ¼ cup raspberries (cut in half)
- 3 white chocolate truffles (cut in quarters)

Directions:
1. In a mixing dish, combine the cream cheese, sugar, and raspberry preserves. Using a whisk, blend all ingredients until they are thoroughly mixed and the sugar begins to dissolve.
2. Combine the heavy whipping cream and milk in a mixing bowl. Whisk until all of the ingredients are thoroughly blended. Because the raspberry preserves mixture is fairly thick, this may take a minute or two.
3. Half of the raspberries, cut in half, should be added. Depending on the size, this should yield 6 to 8 raspberries.
4. Once all ingredients have been added (except the mix-ins), pour into an empty ninja CREAMi Pint container and freeze for 24 hours.
5. After 24 hours, remove the Pint from the freezer. Remove the lid.
6. Place the Ninja CREAMi Pint into the outer bowl. Place the outer bowl with the Pint in it into the ninja CREAMi machine and turn until the outer bowl locks into place. Push the ICE CREAM button. During the ICE CREAM function, the ice cream will mix together and become very creamy.
7. Once the ICE CREAM function has ended, turn the outer bowl and release it from the ninja CREAMi machine.
8. Make a hole in the center of the ice cream with a spoon that runs from top to bottom. The mix-ins will be placed in this hole. Add the ¼ cup of raspberries and 3 white chocolate truffles to the mix. Make sure the raspberries are cut in half, and the truffles are sliced into quarters. Because these mix-ins will not be broken down into smaller bits during the mixing process, you'll want to make sure they're in little chunks.
9. Place the outer bowl with the Pint back into the ninja CREAMi machine and lock it into place. Choose the MIX-IN function.
10. Once the Ninja CREAMi completes the MIX-IN cycle, remove the outer bowl from the machine.
11. Your ice cream is ready to eat! Enjoy!

Nutrition Info:
- InfoCalories 138,Protein 16g,Carbohydrate 121g,Fat 97g,Sodium 246mg.

Cherry-chocolate Chunk Ice Cream

Servings: 4 | Cooking Time: 24 Hours And 10minutes

Ingredients:
- 1 packet frozen sweet cherries
- ¾ cup heavy cream
- 1 can sweetened condensed milk
- ½ cup milk
- 1 teaspoon vanilla extract
- 1 bar semisweet baking chocolate, broken into small chunks

Directions:
1. Combine the heavy cream, sweetened condensed milk, milk, and vanilla extract in a mixing bowl.
2. Pour the ice cream mixture into an empty ninja CREAMi Pint container, add the chopped cherries and chocolate chunks, and freeze for 24 hours.
3. After 24 hours, remove the Pint from the freezer. Remove the lid.
4. Place the Ninja CREAMi Pint into the outer bowl. Place the outer bowl with the Pint in it into the ninja CREAMi machine and turn until the outer bowl locks into place. Push the ICE CREAM button.
5. Once the ICE CREAM function has ended, turn the outer bowl and release it from the ninja CREAMi machine.

Nutrition Info:
- InfoCalories 458,Protein 7.2g,Carbohydrate 48g,Fat 28g,Sodium 92mg.

Low-sugar Vanilla Ice Cream

Servings:4 | Cooking Time:x

Ingredients:
- 1¾ cup fat-free half-and-half
- ¼ cup stevia cane sugar blend
- 1 teaspoon vanilla extract

Directions:
1. In a medium bowl, whisk the half-and-half, sugar, and vanilla together until everything is combined and the sugar is dissolved. The mixture will be foamy. Let it sit for 5 minutes or until the foam subsides.
2. Pour the base into a clean CREAMi Pint. Place the storage lid on the container and freeze for 24 hours.
3. Remove the CREAMi Pint from the freezer and take off the lid. Place the pint in the outer bowl of your Ninja CREAMi, install the Creamerizer Paddle in the outer bowl lid, and lock the lid assembly onto the outer bowl. Place the bowl assembly on the motor base, and twist the handle to the right to raise the platform and lock it in place. Select the Lite Ice Cream function.
4. Once the machine has finished processing, remove the ice cream from the pint. Serve immediately.

Blueberry Ice Cream

Servings: 4 | Cooking Time:x

Ingredients:
- 1 cup blueberries
- ½ cup vanilla whole milk Greek yogurt
- ¼ cup milk
- 2 tablespoons honey
- 2 tablespoons chia seeds

Directions:
1. In a bowl, add all ingredients and eat until well combined.
2. Transfer the mixture into an empty Ninja CREAMi pint container.
3. Cover the container with storage lid and freeze for 24 hours.
4. After 24 hours, remove the lid from container and arrange into the Outer Bowl of Ninja CREAMi.
5. Install the Creamerizer Paddle onto the lid of Outer Bowl.
6. Then rotate the lid clockwise to lock.
7. Press Power button to turn on the unit.
8. Then press Ice Cream button.
9. When the program is completed, turn the Outer Bowl and release it from the machine.
10. Transfer the ice cream into serving bowls and serve immediately.

Nutrition Info:
- InfoCalories: 115,Fat: 4g,Carbohydrates: 19.4g,Protein: 3.1.

Strawberry-carrot Ice Cream

Servings:4 | Cooking Time:x

Ingredients:
- 1 cup frozen carrot slices, thawed
- ½ cup trimmed and quartered fresh strawberries
- 1 tablespoon cream cheese, at room temperature
- ⅓ cup granulated sugar
- 1 teaspoon strawberry extract
- ½ cup whole milk
- 5 drops red food coloring
- ½ cup heavy (whipping) cream

Directions:
1. Combine the carrots, strawberries, cream cheese, sugar, strawberry extract, milk, and food coloring in a blender. Blend on high until smooth.
2. Pour the base into a clean CREAMi Pint. Whisk in the heavy cream until combined. Place the storage lid on the container and freeze for 24 hours.
3. Remove the CREAMi Pint from the freezer and take off the lid. Place the pint in the outer bowl of your Ninja CREAMi, install the Creamerizer Paddle in the outer bowl lid, and lock the lid assembly onto the outer bowl. Place the bowl assembly on the motor base, and twist the handle to the right to raise the platform and lock it in place. Select the Ice Cream function.
4. Once the machine has finished processing, remove the ice cream from the pint. Serve immediately with desired toppings.

Earl Grey Tea Ice Cream

Servings: 4 | Cooking Time: 25 Minutes

Ingredients:
- 1 cup heavy cream
- 1 cup whole milk
- 5 tablespoons monk fruit sweetener
- 3 Earl Grey tea bags

Directions:
1. In a medium saucepan, add cream and milk and stir to combine.
2. Place saucepan over medium heat and cook until for bout two-three minutes or until steam is rising.
3. Stir in the monk fruit sweetener and reduce the heat to very low.
4. Add teabags and cover the saucepan for about 20 minutes.
5. Discard the tea bags and remove saucepan from heat.
6. Transfer the mixture into an empty Ninja CREAMi pint container and place into an ice bath to cool.
7. After cooling, cover the container with storage lid and freeze for 24 hours.
8. After 24 hours, remove the lid from container and arrange into the Outer Bowl of Ninja CREAMi.
9. Install the Creamerizer Paddle onto the lid of Outer Bowl.
10. Then rotate the lid clockwise to lock.
11. Press Power button to turn on the unit.
12. Then press Ice Cream button.
13. When the program is completed, turn the Outer Bowl and release it from the machine.
14. Transfer the ice cream into serving bowls and serve immediately.

Nutrition Info:
- InfoCalories: 140,Fat: 13.1g,Carbohydrates: 3.6g,Protein: 2.6.

Servings: 4 | Cooking Time: 10 Seconds

Ingredients:
- 1 tablespoon cream cheese, softened
- ⅓ cup granulated sugar
- 2 tablespoons matcha powder
- 1 teaspoon vanilla extract
- 1 cup whole milk
- ¾ cup heavy cream

Directions:
1. In a large microwave-safe bowl, add the cream cheese and microwave for on High for about ten seconds.
2. Remove from the microwave and stir until smooth.
3. Add the sugar, matcha powder and vanilla extract and with a wire whisk, beat until the mixture looks like frosting.
4. Slowly add the milk and heavy cream and beat until well combined.
5. Transfer the mixture into an empty Ninja CREAMi pint container.
6. Cover the container with storage lid and freeze for 24 hours.
7. After 24 hours, remove the lid from container and arrange into the Outer Bowl of Ninja CREAMi.
8. Install the Creamerizer Paddle onto the lid of Outer Bowl.
9. Then rotate the lid clockwise to lock.
10. Press Power button to turn on the unit.
11. Then press Ice Cream button.
12. When the program is completed, turn the Outer Bowl and release it from the machine.
13. Transfer the ice cream into serving bowls and serve immediately.

Nutrition Info:
- InfoCalories: 188,Fat: 11.2g,Carbohydrates: 20.3g,Protein: 2.6.

Mocha Ice Cream

Servings: 4 | Cooking Time:x

Ingredients:
- ½ cup mocha cappuccino mix
- 1¾ cups coconut cream
- 3 tablespoons agave nectar

Directions:
1. In a bowl, add all ingredients and beat until well combined.
2. Transfer the mixture into an empty Ninja CREAMi pint container.
3. Cover the container with storage lid and freeze for 24 hours.
4. After 24 hours, remove the lid from container and arrange into the Outer Bowl of Ninja CREAMi.
5. Install the Creamerizer Paddle onto the lid of Outer Bowl.
6. Then rotate the lid clockwise to lock.
7. Press Power button to turn on the unit.
8. Then press Ice Cream button.
9. When the program is completed, turn the Outer Bowl and release it from the machine.
10. Transfer the ice cream into serving bowls and serve immediately.

Nutrition Info:
- InfoCalories: 297,Fat: 25.4g,Carbohydrates: 19.2g,Protein: 2.5.

Appendix : Recipes Index

L

M

O

P

Made in United States
Troutdale, OR
06/07/2023